Loving You All Year Wrong

By

Brett Banjo

January

I Don't Mind
(New Year's Day)

Loving you
Cause they say
What you do
On New Year's day
You'll do all year
Which is why
I keep trying
To put it in your ear
Cause baby
There's something
I want you to hear
It sounds like a whisper
As I draw near
Then it will boom
And thunder
All the way to your brain
Leaving no room to wonder
How what started
As a simple grind
Has left me
Always
On your mind

Labotorgasmic

I love you
For your mind
That's why
I put it
In
Your eye
What I'm after
Is what you think
Watch out brain
Here comes dink

Treasure Versus Strain

Loving you
I lost the bet
He said shiny
I said wet
But the only part
That I regret
Is doubling-down
Ongoing down
To initiate another round
He said airplane
I said jet
The other part
That I regret
Never bet
With your own pet
It really strains the relationship

Bound Buy Bags

Loving you
Through a hole
That I made
In the bag
Makes me look
Like I'm mad
But I'm really just sad
That the hole
In the bag
Has started
To chafe
Just at the time
That I found
The right place
To love you
Where you're bound
In the sack
That I found
When there was none
But us
Around
And I knew
I loved you
More
Than could ever be found
In a bag on the ground
Unless that love
Was properly bound

My Better Half is Always the Second

Dreams
Are the curse
Of the young
Despair
Is the life
Of the married
But it doesn't have to be that
way
Once
The spouse
Is buried
You always said you were going
to leave
So I'm the one that they'll believe
And ever since
You went away
I've been getting laid
By all your friends
Who feel a need
To comfort me
And all agree
Down to the letter
They always thought
I could do better

Done the Salisbury Steak and Ready for Cobbler

Just because
I'm married
Doesn't mean
My loves not real
I still love desert
Even if I've had a meal
What I lack in smooth
I make up for in zeal
Go ahead
Grab a rubber
Pick any flavor
Personally
I like vanilla
That's what I use
When alone
And dressed like Cinderella
If you've ever wanted
To be an evil stepsister
Now's your big chance
Or maybe
You'd rather
Start
Our first date
With a dance

Bring Out the Lotion

Bald
Baby
You're a doll
Holes
In your arteries
Lines
Cross your wrists
I got gingivitis
When we shared
Our first kiss
And that itch
You gave me
From the gnats
Crab
And mice
Are not a
Pestilence
But an exotic
Spice
Baby
I'm thank full
For everything
You've given
I'm walking in a cloud
Living in a dream
But mostly I'm thankful
For anti-itch cream

Never Judge a Race by the Blackout

Loving you
After you downed
The whole drink
Even though
The pills
Turned your gin pink
Leaving you still
And thoughtless
Hours of thrills
Without risk
Lay ahead
When I'm through
I'll drag you
Out of my bed
And dump you
In the ghetto
Where you'll remember the
crime
But my face
You will lack
And you'll point your finger
At some unfortunate black
You always hated
That race
Without walking a mile
Wearing their face
So don't look for sympathy
We all agree
You're a disgrace
You disgust me
They should put you away
And throw away the cell
Needless to say
I'll see you in hell

Shy Guy

Loving you
Through a hole
That I dug in my bed
Through the mattress
Past the frame
So I can peak
At your head
Where you lay
On the floor
On the boards
Where you lay
With your head
By your feet
And your feet by my head
With a bind
And a gag
So you can't see my face
And can't speak to my ear
Even though I lie near
Longing to hear
While I lie
By the hole
Just above
The girl that I love
If only I could find a way
To seal the deal
And tell her
Exactly
How I feel

Props to the Goddess

Ha la lue yah
I love god
Each
And every
Night
He comes in late
Yells and bites
And smells a lot like whiskey
Likes to lick and kick
And doesn't want to kiss me
Now I love god
As much as any other
But if he doesn't start behaving
I'm gonna tell his mother

Parting the Parts

Loving you
For your feet
They're the only part
I'm gonna keep
But you can have
The shoes
Concentrate
On what you got
Not what you're gonna lose
It will make things easier
When we part
If you thank your lucky star
I never loved your heart

Putting the Special In Delivered

Loving you
As you come
Through the door
It don't really matter
If I'd seen you before
I don't really see you now
I look only long enough
To get you to the ground
And we rolled
And we rolled
Round
And around
And when we stopped
Joy is found
Oh postman
Don't you see
My message to you
Is your message to me
I hope you enjoyed
This special
Delivery

Taking Out the Twins

Don't take it
Personally
I slept
With your
Other
Personality
You didn't tell me
When we met
That you came as a set
Maybe I should not have
assumed
But you were naked
In my room
On the bed
And didn't use your mouth
Much for talking
Let's get this thing a rockin'
Is the only thing you said
Best thing ever
In and out of that head
And I'll do it again
Then I'd do it again
Sorry for the repetition
But between you and her
God
There's no competition
You're a lap dog
And she's a hottie
You're uptight
And she's so naughty
It's amazing
How much better
She looks
Wearing
Your body

Stuck Between Sticking and Stiff

Loving you
Bound to you
Stuck to you
Loving glue
Sticky white
My delight
The only love I can recall
I let you thicken
In my hands
Then roll you in a ball
That goes
In my nose
Numbing me
Right to my toes
Which is what I really love
If you must know
If you must hear
What's really true
But do me a favor
And don't tell glue

Run Yum Run

Yum
Plus
Yum
Equals
Yum yum
That's how I feel
Since we included
Your mom
The two of you
Are one hell of a ride
And only one of you
Can get pregnant
So while
You used to be
My only one
Now
I'm just aiming
For your bum

Secret Herbs and Seasonings

I'd love
To love
A chicken
That'd be finger lickin'
And the gravy'd be divine
She'd be round
And feathered
I'd be bound
And tethered
How the seasoning would fly
And before we are through
I'll make you
Cock-a-doodle-doo
Till you feel
You're Kentucky fried

Lover of Another Color
(Martin Luther King Day)

Loving you
You're not my color
I'd stick to my own
But life would be duller
I don't want to be alone
And I won't persecute you
I don't have hate
I have a bone
I want to hammer my way
through you
Setting you on fire
With desire
A romping wild toss
Always beats a burning cross
Hate
Ain't
A part of how I date
Unless you're ugly
Which should be a race of its
own
One we all can agree
Should be left alone
Shunned and repressed
Now that's good prejudice
But hot knows no race
If you got a nice face
And ain't all stretched out
From being a mother
Or sleeping with brothers
Not that I mind
A man that's black
I'm just way too small
To follow that act

Seven Ate Nine

Three beers
Five shots
A couple lines of coke
When I say
I love you
You act like it's a joke
Three more beers
Five more shots
A big fat toke of weed
Tell your friends
The man is here
It's time
To do the deed
Bring a pitcher
Leave the bottle
A bump of heroin
How's your mother
What the fuck
I like hairy men
Do you have a brother
What are you looking at
Those aren't my pants
There on my head
Which must make them my hat
Bar tend bring another
I'm still able to mutter
Next thing I know
I wake up
In the gutter

Something or Something

Love
Suites me
Like
A
Suite
Or something
I
Love you
Like
Potato
Dumplings
I'm not
As good
At words
As I am
With a shovel
Baby
You're the only one
I'm ever gonna
Lovel

Get Ye Behind Me

I keep you close
Close to my heart
My dear
But even closer
To my rear
Bending over
To lend you an ear
I can hear
You there
Gasping for air
Don't mess with a man
With a giant ass
It's a hell of a place
To take your last gasp

Originally Yours

I could love you
Forever
But that would be cliché
It's much more original
If we loved
For just four days
Then you'd be hip and cool
I'd be witty and funny
There'd be no time to act the fool
And I'll save a lot of money
Never growing tired
Of what I've already had
If you look at it you'll see
The deal really ain't that bad
You'll be free of me
After tasting all I've got
Long before it occurs to you
It's really not a lot
And I'll be rid of you

Ring a Ding a Ling

She's got rings
On her fingers
Rings on her crotch
Rings on her nipples
Rings on her socks
Rings on her pimples
Her brow and her nose
Her cheek and her rear
Her elbows and her toes
She has rings
Everyplace
She has rings
Everywhere
But when I lean on her bell
She's never there

Using You Using Me

Baby
You're worth a million
But all I got is twenty
Fortunately
With a rock of crack
That's plenty
To make you feel like a million
For several minutes
More than I will need
It ain't about love
It's all about speed
Which is exactly the thing
We both desire
For that
You've got my back
As I hump yours
Sharing what decent folk lack
Not letting go
Till once again
We both feel
Like crap

Taking You for Granite

I never knew
How much
I loved you
Till you told me
You were leaving
I can't think of anything
You have
But rather
What you lack
Seems
I don't love you
Much at all
Let me help you pack

As Hot As You

Your body
Is like heaven
It's a place
Where people
Who don't know how to have
fun
End up
Just my luck
I finally found
A girl to do
And I'd be better off
Humping a puck
At least it knows
How to score
And spends less time
Looking bored
Never yawns
With disdain
Asking if I need some more
Who would ever
Want to be with you
Oh that's right
I do
Your loving may lack fever
But I'm really not
That hot either

Am I the Animal I Am

If I were a ferocious lover
I'd be a tiger under cover
If I were a dog inside
I'd keep my eye on the prize
But when I'm in bed
I choose the monkey instead
They're loose and they're limber
With opposable thumbs
With more tricks and hijinks
To get the job done
Jumping up and down
Bouncing all around
And just when you think
I've shown you all I got
I'll thrill you with a loop de loop
Always wishing
I could stop
Before
I threw
The poop

All In Fall Out

Loving you
Is in the pot
I've just got to meet the anti
All I have left is my wife
And once she's in
I begin to wonder
If I should win
Are you really worth
Winning my wife
Or should I fold
And run for my life
I think about it a little bit more
As I'm headed out the door

Digging You

Loving you
Like the squirrel
That tried so hard to burrow
When it saw me running naked
in the yard
But a squirrel cannot burrow
It finds it way too hard
It would be better off climbing a
tree
That's the best way
To escape naked me
Underground
Only makes me
A little more eager
For somewhere in that squirrel
Is a really sweet beaver
That wouldn't be afraid of me
If it were safe in a tree
But if you're stuck underground
And you can't turn around
And you're barely as big as my
fist
There is nothing you can do
It's over
You're through
Just like it happened to the
squirrel
Though I love you just the same

All That's Brown is Not Gold

Bells rang
Birds flew
The sun set
I said those two words
I'd been wanting to say
Ever since the day we met
Eat turds
Then I hit you
With a cow patty
Wrapped around a rock
To think I used to call you daddy
Let your key inside my lock
Now I'm back
You're just Bob
And that million-dollar smile
Won't be worth a quarter
To hell with the restraining order

3 Out of 10

I love you more
Than at least three of my toes
Be quiet about it
I don't want them to know
They're a major part
Of wherever I go
And if they knew
I loved you more
They'd never bring me
Near your door
Which gives me a great out
As soon as I think
This love is beat
And you aren't the one
That I want to meet
I'll just blame it
On my feet

February

Anonymity Have a Drink on Me

Loving you
Though you've puked
All over my pants
Loving you
Cause when you're sober
I don't stand a chance
And I don't care
That you think
My name is Berney
And I don't care
That I'll probably
Cum way to early
And I don't care
That tomorrow
Your brothers
Will show up at my door
If that is
You remember
What happened the night before
So before I go
We'll have one last drink
And in your mind
I'll never be
Exactly who you think

Shadow Gets You Six (Groundhogs Day)

I've waited
Patiently
All night
By your hole
You're whom I love
And silently stole
Simple trick
Some cheese on a stick
Threw you in a bag
And got out of there quick
I don't give a shit
For a shadow
Weeks of winter
Weeks of spring
Don't mean a thing
Cause I'm gonna make
This groundhog sing

Two Heads Are Better Than a Bird in the Hand

I
Can get
Head
But head
Can't
Get me
I can fill one up
And set one free
Only good thing
About being me
I've got two heads
And one's empty

Put Some Fruit in that Shake

Loving you
I'm a real lucky fellow
You remind me
Of a bowl full of Jell-O
I can see the fruit
In you jiggle
Whenever
Your air filled head
Lets out a giggle
You're the lover
There's no stopping
You look great
With whipped topping
There's always room
For you
But the part
That I like best
Is you're gone
When we're through

Strings Attached

Loving you
With a string
That's attached
To my thing
When I'm good
You can thrill me
When I'm bad
You could kill me
Somewhere in-between
I'll do whatever you say
Walk me around
Make me sit
Make me beg
Just be careful
The way
You pull on my head
It's already
Starting
To turning deep blue
One way
Or another
I'll soon
Be through

Two Times Baby

Loving you
At seven
And eleven
That's July
And November
So don't be in such a hurry
It's only half past February

Morning Would

Loving you
Twice
Before you're awake
Without even having
To look at your face
Cause girl
You sleep like a rock
Without even stirring
When as I drove in my cock
You didn't budge at all
Could I be that small
That you find my prowess
No more than a pin
I huff
And I puff
But you're still
Sleeping in

If You Would Like to Know How Much I Love You I Recommend Asking the Dog

Loving you
Enough
For four lines
And one rhyme

Cold Ass Love

Will you be
My polar bear
I love
Seal meat
I love
Club feet
I love
The way you bite
And tear
In a land
Where night
Last a long ass time
I'd lose someone small
Less likely to maul
And I know
To you
I'm emergency food
But if we keep finding meat
One day you'll find me so sweat
Our love
You won't want to eat
It won't be worth the hurt
And I'll be saved
At least 'til desert

After, What I'm after, After

Loving you
With plaster
So I can keep
What I'm after
Forever
Recreating my love
Out of rawhide
Leather
With a touch of lotion
So the motion
Won't chaff
And you'll remain safe
From the kind of crackin'
That will ruin the action
And leave me
No love to embrace
Cause god knows
The first thing I'll wear out
Is gonna be your face

Faster Than Crass

Loving you
So damn fast
That if I were
To pass
Some gas
Down by your toes
I'd be done
With your ass
Before the smell
Could reach
Your nose

Sing Sweet Mocking Bird Thing

I wrote you a song
It starts with some crap
Mostly about love
And ends
With a smack
Across my face
Breaking the flow
Ruining the pace
I meant fat pig in a good way
Don't be sore
Don't go away
There's still another verse
I haven't gotten to the part
That's supposed to hurt
In a good way
The kind of honest
That gets me laid
But you go home
And I'm alone
Which really
Ruins
The happy ending

Love Rolls On While I Walk

Loving you
With the wheel
From my bike
It never got me real far
But you
It seems to like
And you look good
Together
I can see
You two
Going places
But I can't keep up
The pace
I feel I'm going nowhere
And you're already gone
And the wheel
It got you there
And I see
I'm no longer needed
I pack the frame of my bike
And I beat it

Hearts in a Candy Shaped Box
(Valentine's Day)

A heart
Full of confections
Reminds me
Of the affection
We shared
Before the infection
And the loss
Of your hair
That changed
The direction
Our love would take
Or was it always
Only
Fake
When you're from a small town
There's only
So many places
Disease can be found
Sadly
You found yours next door
I warned you about my step-
daddy
You should have let him be
After promising yourself to me
But you cheated
Right from the start
So try and be glad
I only
Took
Your heart

The Banana Points Away

I met her at the fair
Little buggies in her hair
She ooked and acked
And stole my heart
I have found
My other part
Stay with me
Monkey please
Stay with me
She came
And went
Leaving me
With just her scent
That I kept in a bag
Full of kinky
Buggy hair
Let her go
Monkey show
Let her go
Locked inside a monkey car
So very, very monkey far
So very far away from me
Speeding on a monkey train
Filling me with monkey pain
I can't go on
Monkey gone
Can't go on
That's all there is to say
I lean against the empty cage
Empty, clean and critter free
Disinfected just like me
I cry a long low monkey cry
Cursing the god of monkey sky
I'm so alone
No monkey home

I'm so alone
I'll never feel her grisly fur
I'll never smell her monkey
breath
Or supple sticky monkey breast
For me
There's really nothing left

Gold Miner's Pick

Loving you
Ain't that bad
My parents believe
I'm no longer a fag
They even seems glad
When I say
We'll have grandkids someday
As soon as you get off the rag
So it isn't that bad
Loving Nick
A beautiful girl
Who used to be Rick
And when she unpacks
She still has her dick
Which is way better
Than when I could only
masturbate
Afraid I'd get caught
On a date
Get cut off
Lose the estate
This way we all get what I want
And no one has to die
This time

Got the Time

Tick tock
Loving you
Round the clock
Behind the clock
Through the clock
God we're locked
But you haven't seen me
I've been stealthy
So I have time
Time to figure out
How to get out
Of this mess
Your arms pinned back
Behind your dress
With me
Holding on
For far too long
Behind the clock
All soft cock
And ready to blow
But if I let go
Then you'll know
I really need
To start thinking
Things through
This is no way
For me
To get
To know you

When Floor Meets Door

Baby I swear
We're
Halfway there
It just the beer
I'm getting close
But nowhere near
So let's be clear
My core
Needs more
Of things I can't get at the store
We can't do it on my own
Let's both pretend
That you're alone
While I take
A near lethal mix
A narcotic fix
To get me off the floor
If I can get
All of this
Before you reach the door
I'll be up
And you'll be down
Enough in me for a double
round
But if you get to the door
Before
Then I'll just give it
To the floor

Termination Before the Call

Loving you
Before you know
What you're doing
Leaving you
Before you know
What we did
Is for the best
Leaves the least mess
I'm just another
Vague kind of lover
That didn't impress
I didn't come to conquer
I just stopped for a rest
Lost to time
Lost in your mind
Like the guy
Who almost discovered America
You don't dream
Of a man
You can barely remember
A vague notion
From a blurred bender
You'll never bother me
Won't interfere with my life
You're just another phone call
That won't reach my wife

An Abe Bodied Man
(Presidents Day)

To celebrate
President's day
I decided
To love you
Many ways
More than Washington would
More than Lincoln could
If I want to have fun
I'm gonna need me Hamilton
Fistfuls of the man
That I'll stuff
Into your hand
And into your pants
That president sure has a way
Of getting you to dance
I don't know much about him
Other than he's green
Used to be President
And in such high demand
I can't pay my rent
I can't believe
Such a high-powered man
Would so flagrantly break the
law
It must be a kink
Call it a flaw
Say that he's sick
Or just doesn't care
But Hamilton
Loves
Your underwear

The Best Sucks Less

Unfortunately
You're the best
And I've looked
And looked
Discarding the rest
And just my luck
Even you suck
But you suck less
Making you the very best
Unfortunately
I suck more
Right down to
My sucking core
I could never get
Anyone
That sucks as much
As you
What's a man
That sucks
To do

Some Beats None

Loving you
For one more line
Maybe two
I'll love you to death
I've always been true
I can't stand your breath
I can't stand you face
Baby
Get out
We are through

French, Fry, and Mash Me

Baby
You're my sweet tomato
I love you
Dearly
And Nearly
As much
As a damn fine potato
Cause baby we have fun
What I love
More than you
Are just the greatest ones
Like hash-browns
Or fries
So baby don't cry
I love you way more
Than sweet potatoes
Ten times more than yams
Baby you're the girl for me
But I am only
A man
That loves you
Equal too
Instant potatoes
With lots of butter and salt
Your eyes are cool shimmering
lakes
That makes you better
Than potato pancakes
And I love your long silky hair
So I won't bring up chips
Cause baby that ain't fare
But twice baked potatoes
With your sweet lips
You're better than those
Cause baby you're hot
But baby
You ain't no tatter tot

Time Flies and Then You Marry One

Loving you
With an apple
Ever since you got sick
But all of the slices
Haven't
Helped you a bit
With fruit flies enough
To sound like a hive
We joke that
Since they're living inside
They make you less nearly dead
And more nearly alive
But I'm afraid
That soon you're going to die
And all I'll have left
Is that hive
And those flies
Which I've been calling Betty
I've introduced her to the kids
I have to be ready
She'll be my second wife
She's a lot like you
I have to go on with my life
What do you mean
I want you sick
How can you say
I want you dead
Oh drink your Lysol
And get back in bed

Insert Slot A into Slit C

Insert name here
And I
Sitting in a deforested zone
Exchanging a mutual
Form
Of herpes
First comes tongue
Then comes diarrhea
Then the cancer
Sets in
The end

Unless they cut your ass off in time
In which case
No end

Lone Wolf

Loving you
Makes me sick
Loving you
Makes me vomit
If I were a wolf
I'd eat you
Right up to your bonnet
Then the hair-balls
I cough
And the bones
That pass through
I'll rebuild
In a way
That reminds me
Of you

Forget You Ever Knew Me
For at Least Two Minutes

Loving you
Like tomorrow
I'm the man
Who never comes
Loving you
Like a shark
That's worn down
To the gums
Used to be
Yesterday
But all that is over
Used to be
The alpha dog
But now
I'm barely Rover
Sorry
To say
I gotta role you over
And could you please
Scream
Who's there
So I won't be so shy
We'll both get off
Much better
Pretending
I'm another guy

It Never Hurts to Try

Loving you
Or your sister
Whichever one
Delivers quicker
Call it competition
The winners the one
That loves me the most often
It might make me sound
A little bit rotten
But maybe
It would help me
Decide
If you threw in a brother
The dainty one
He'd like a ride
And then your mother
Who dead asleep
By two drinks
And won't stir
If I don't go deep
And I won't
Well I can't
But we'll save that
For another rant
I still need to get you
Out of those pants
Don't resist
You're no fighter
It will just take a second
I brought my lighter

Embrace

Loving you
From the first time
I held you
Down
You screamed
Let me up
I yelled
Please don't drown
You gasped
Get the hell off
I said
Watch out for the ground
Then a flip and a flop
And you were on top
Your hands on my throat
I swore I was done
You smiled
And slapped me
Saying
We've just begun

March

Long Long Long Long Long LongTime

Loving you
Like a toaster
I'll put it in
And you make it black
For everything I'm not good at
There's something I lack
So I'm asking you
To act
Like I'm supper bad
In the sack
And I'll make it worth
The grown
And the smile
I won't call you again
For a long
Long
Long
While

Hay Now

Loving you
Under the hay
Quietly
Till your dad
Goes away
With his gun
But don't worry
I won't run
Not until
The job
Is done

Grace From the Staircase

Love
Is a gift
From above
That's where
Mrs. Walkins lives
From whom
All blessings
Flow
At least
As long
As her husband
Don't know

With You I Dream of Family

You I am lovin'
Like you are my cousin
Full of fear we'll get caught
Doing what we ought not
In a love so deep
Only family can reach
Unless family reaches you first
Tearing you from limb to
pimples
Describing a baby
With a brain so simple
Despite its two heads
That can't get along
Three arms
One leg
And a twin for a thong
And it won't be long
Till Grandma finds out
Then look out
Get out
Run for the hills
If she gets her hands on you
She's going to kill
What a rush
What a thrill
It's just what I need
To imagine
When make love
In any fashion
So please don't lose your head
When it's not your name
I call in bed
It's you that I'm lovin'
While dreaming
I just

Got caught
With my cousin

Lost On My Lips

I don't mean to be rude
But I ain't in the mood
I have an infection
That covers my brain
That says more of the same
Won't lead to reaction
I appreciate all you do
And the number of times
You've done it
So it isn't you
It's me
Somewhere
Between
My beef
And my brain
My lips have grown tired of
Calling your name

All's Well in Hell's Hell

There is a place
I keep my love
That you will never find
You see I left no trail
Or evidence behind
She's mine
She's mine
She's mine she's mine
She's mine she's mine she's mine
And if I burn in hell for this
I really do not mind
True love is worth sacrifice
True love is worth sacrilege
And if god can't understand
Then he didn't put the heart in
man
And if there is no love in heaven
Then hell is full of love
And I'll run into my sweaty
there
Just like I did above
She's the only one for me
My only true desire
That's why I'll burry her again
Down by the lake of fire
And if hell
Has a hell
I'll be headed there as well

Long Handle

Loving you
With a rake
That I found
In the yard
It's not as hard
As it's long
And the love
Was all wrong
Till I went to the right
Rake
Rake
Delight
A joy like no other
And when we're done
I'll cleaned your gutter

Too Many Pillows

Loving you
Like I care
Like I know
You are there
Like my eyes
Are not closed
Like you not just a hole
Not a sign
Or a shake
Not a noise do you make
So I pretend I'm through
And I fake that I blew
Swearing you never were better
That you did nothing wrong
I stare at the pillow
And silently wonder
How long you've been gone

To the Tip of My Trunk

Loving you
Like a man
That I met
In the park
In his pants was a bulge
In his eyes were a spark
I hit him on the head
When we were near
Where I parked
I dropped him in my trunk
Alone in the dark
Alone only if
You don't count the others
A collection of sorts
That includes one of my brothers
A dozen young men
Piled on top of each other
Like they though they'd be on
me
I laugh when I think they have
nowhere to pee
Ironic for men that I commonly
see
In bathrooms
In parks
All across the country
Leering at me
When I'm trying to go
When I'm trying to pee
They're leering at me
So I can't seem to go
And they look at me
Like the reason they know
But it's not what they think
And it ain't what they thunk

Which is why I collect them
And keep them in my trunk
So the world will be free
Of anyone
That makes it harder to pee
Cause life is hard enough
already

Out of the Box with No Place to Go

Loving you
In a cabin
Way up in the wood
Where there's no place
To run to
Even if you could
Not that I'm such a bad guy
I did remove the hood
And the duct tape
From your eyes
And I pulled you
From the crate
Which is more
Than most would do
For a newly
Purchased
Mate

Tender

Loving you
With a love
Tender as a dove
That's been pounded
And marinated correctly
Baked
And basted
In fat that's its own
Till it's flesh
Nearly falls
Right off of the bone
So moist
And so tender
Just like the way
I'm gonna love you
Forever

Swampy Where it Counts

Loving you
I'm a smooth operator
Loving you
You're real slow
For a gator
Out in the bayou
Ain't much to do
And if I can get the dress on
You'll look like my ma
In the very best of her moo-moos

Rock 'em, Cock 'em

Loving you
With a rock
Just the size
Of my cock
So you'll never know
And I won't be exposed
To the monster inside
That makes me shrink
Makes me hide
Like a possum
Playing dead
In the road
Or a sausage
Left out
In the cold
That's why I keep it dark
That's why I use this stone
I love you with all my heart
But I'm afraid what you got
May just melt my bone

Snow No Boundaries

Loving you
Has left me cold
What once was hot
Has gotten old
You'd always do
Whatever I'd say
Molding you
Like fresh wet clay
That's what I like
About a girl
Made of snow
I left out the mouth
So you cannot say no
Leaving me
To my delight
Till the final blow
When I found out
What you're really liked
No mouth for a kiss
But you still got teeth
When you clamp down
I can't fight
My best parts
Crumble
From your frost bite

Out of that World

Loving you
Like I would
If I thought
That I could
But I can't
So I don't
Except by remote
Where I am not me
And you are not you
And the computer controls
All that we do
In that world I am great
But you're second rate
So don't be surprised
When there's no second date

It's Like a Threesome Cause You're Both Fucked

Loving you
Without a clue
Neither I
Nor you
And as I fly
Into the night
Neither of us
Will remember the flight
Or anything that we did
Leaves very little
About me
That you can tell
Our kid

The Day I Met Shoe

Loving you
You're the closest
To the bar door
I need something to grab
As I fall to the floor
Meeting your shoe
Which I cling desperately to
Dragging you down
As I'm thrown
From the bar
With no other girl
Have I gotten so far
I climb to your ear
Through drool
And through vomit
I whisper to you
I live really near
But whatever you answered
Was not very clear
And now you are gone
Forever I fear
Despite my insistence
For love I would stay
The police still showed up
To take me away

When Irish Eyes are Blackened (St Patrick's Day)

Green
Makes me horny
Whiskey
Makes me mean
Green colored liquor
Leaves me
Somewhere
In between
When I saw you
On my bar stool
I almost punched
You in the head
Then green eyes
Fluttered at me
And I wanted you instead
That's when
You hit me
And I knew that it was love
We went to the back alley
For a roll in the mud
Me
You
And a flask
A kiss so deep
A punch in the ribs
Then a kick in the ass
It gets hazy from there
Just what we did
But one things for sure
We'll have really tough kids

Till the Break of Day

Loving you
In a way
That I'm not proud
I shot for funky
Aimed for kinky
But only managed loud
It's not me
It's not you
It's not the best I can do
The fault isn't mine
Oh
Fine
It is me
And I can't do any better
I've a wee-wee pee-pee
And I'm a bed wetter
I should have come with a sign
No matter how hard you try
There'll be no joy
Till morning
When you can finally leave
Without a scene
Without me crying
My tears don't flow
When the sun's shinning

Passing Through

Loving you
In the drive through
Where I know abuse
Is nothing new
Thank you sir
May I have another
If you're gonna hit me like that
I'll start calling you mother
You're a disgrace
A waste
Not worth the mace
And that's not a laugh
It's a cackle
If you don't like it
Get a gag
And some shackles
I ain't gonna stop ya
I'll be waiting in my car
Bring my fries
And your Whopper
Then we'll lay
A patch of tar

Mop on Top

I made love
To a mop
That I called
By your name
Might seem strange
But the sex
Was the same

That Hole's Not Whole

I'm not a friend
I'm just a guy
That ogles lightly at your thighs
Whip me up
And you will find
I never cared
I only lied
I got a higher stake
Scoring you's
A piece of cake
It's a part of my disease
I want a drink
A heavy drought
Of whatever's bound to please
My left side is falling
My right is on the rise
I want the hole
In perception's wall
The falls between your lies

Plowing the Fields

Loving you
Gofer hole
Like I'm a dirty
Little mole
And Farmer Joe
Turned on
The hose

Melts in Your Pants

I got a pussy
Right here
I got it in my pocket
I'm not just braggin'
I've made it out of chocolate
Sweat enough to make your eyes
Double in size
Popping right out of their
sockets
This pussy chocolate
In my pocket
Guaranteed to please
To light your rocket
Rocket socket
Pussy chocolate
Guaranteed to please
Your pocket

Not the Dream I Life

In my dreams
You've found another
Taken on
Another lover
When you tell me
I am free
That's what makes it a dream
And not reality
Where you're not putting out
For anyone
In particular
Everyone gets some
Everyone but me
And I don't have
The strength to flee

Perfect

Lots of people
Know how to read
I'm glad you're not one of them
Lots of people
Have things they believe
I'm glad that's not for you
Our love is so near perfect
I fear it can't be true
I fear you will change
That you'll wake up someday
And ask me my name
Making me tell hospital staff
There's damage to your brain
Cause if they found out
I'm not your husband
They'd tie me high
With a short cord
For conjugal visits
To the comma ward
And for the threesome with your
roommate
They'd throw away the key
After slamming the door
Leaving me
With men
That would beat me to the floor
Loving me
Like a comma patient
Or some discarded pelt
So just like you
I won't know
Exactly how it felt

Erasing You Tomorrow

Loving you
Through electrodes
Attached to my brain
Isn't as lame
As it seems
Cause if feels
Just the same
And we scream
The right names
Which must mean it's real
For I scream
What I feel
And felt
What I screamed
Which can only mean
We are through
I regret
I ever
Downloaded you

Lay Away Paid Tomorrow Not Today

Tomorrow
I will find love
And it won't cost me a dime
For I paid in advance
For a sweet little number
That's gonna be all mine
Shipped here from France
New France
Mexico
Where the men are men
And the women go
For a fair price
But I'm ready
For love
Today
So once again
I'll have to pay

I've Only Changed My Wallet

I'm just as chubby
And as ugly
As you remember
Back when you swore
You'd love me forever
And I still have that problem
With my member
But now I'm wealthy
And can afford better
A girl who doesn't mind
The comments and stares
A girl who'll pretend
She really cares
Cause baby
The price is right
They'll even fain
Pure delight
Everyday
And every night
For the whole 5 minutes

What's Breast For Us Both

Loving you
Though a car
Has run over
Your face
Beauty is a journey
Loves not a race
And I don't mind
How the dogs
Left your chest
My dad always said
A breast is a breast
Is a breast
Is a breast
Is a breast is a breast
Is a breast is a breast
Is a breast is a breast is a breast
Is a breast is a breast is a breast is
a breast is a breast
I'm sure there is more
But I forgot the rest

Honey Bear Underwear

Loving you
With a nest of bees
You always said
You need
Lots of pricks
At least
That's how
You justified it to me
So I figure I'd give you a little
help
Spread your legs
And open your mouth
What they lack in size
They make up in hive
When they're through
I'll have something
Better than love
Better than money
My cheating wife
Will finally be
Sweat as honey

April

A Fool for You
(April Fool's Day)

It took me this long
To open up
I had to make sure
I love you enough
Understand
That for me
This is really tough
I'm not good with my emotions
But I couldn't love you more
With a thousand potions
You've touched me in ways
I didn't know I could feel
And it may sound gay
But I'm closing the deal
To me
You are
Everything
It's time
That finger
Had a ring
Which officially breaks
All of my rules
And by the way
April fool's

Afraid of the Unload

Loving you
Under fire
Heightens my desire
But your daddies
Aim
Is way too good
He ain't huntin' squirrel
He's aiming for wood
I'd love
To love you
But I can't stay
I want to live to love
Another day
Before my wood
Gets shot away

Hay Day

Loving you
The old-time way
I held you
Down
In the hay
Then ran away
But really
It was just in fun
No real harm done
So when we get home
Please
Don't tell mom

A Girl Like Mom Who's Dead

Loving you
I swear
Is a bad idea
Here's some of the reasons why
You smell like pee
Not your own
Weevils have gnawed
You down to the bone
I'd jump in a sewer
If you'd leave me alone
Your hairs
Growing hairs
You look like a bear
Or something the bear
Has eaten
Your face would look better
If thoroughly beaten
You look like you've scratched
And clawed
Your way
Out of a grave
Where you were long ago buried
I can hardly wait
Till we're happily married

Whiskey and the Road

Cheers to you
Flask through
Train-train swirling
Train-train swishing
Little girl
Drunken hurl
Wallet missing

A Drop Then the Bucket

Loving you
With five gallons
Of wine
The whole five gallons
All at one time
Shared
Through a sippy-straw
Feeling divine
Feeling nothing
Too drunk to tell
Where I begin
And where you end
And then
We vomit
And slide
Off of each other
What more can I say
I'm the world's greatest lover

Resurrection (Good Friday)

Loving you
Religiously
Which is why
I nailed you
In three places
Feel free
To be
Exhausted
You have just been saved
Now don't expect me to rise
Again
For at least
Three days

Swingers

Loving you
With a bat
Crack
I told the cops
I was chasing a rat
It leaped on your head
And that was that

If You Love It Cover It with
Chocolate
(Easter)

Loving you
With a rabbit
I pulled from my pocket
Meticulously dipped
In the darkest of chocolate
But still with
Plenty of kick
Have a bite
Take a lick
He won't
Hurt
You a bit
Unless that's
What you're after
He's not that big
But built to dig
And if he burrows too deep
At least
You know
He's yours
To keep

I Ling a Long of Love

Loving you
Cause I love
All the wrong things
And baby
That's everything
You have to bring
You hurt me
So often
So deep
I could sing
La la la
Lo la lo
Ding
A ling
A ling
A ling
Everyone knows
You're a slut
Every knows
You're a stealer
Your mother's on crack
And you are her dealer
You laugh while it's hard
You cackle when I'm limp
Your grandmother's a whore
Your granddad's her pimp
I couldn't love you more
You gave me syphilis
You're so rancid
Baby
I've named you
Bliss
Now come over here
And give daddy a kiss

Balls About Around

It was late
Late last fall
When I first noticed
Extra balls
Growing
Growing out of me
It got to be
So many
Too many
For one man
To carry
I started giving
Them away
One here
Two there
Enough to fill
Every pair of underwear
From here
To the sea
And lately
All the kids I meet
Looks like me

Banana Hand

Loving you
After the puppet show
I've seen you laugh
Always in the front row
The cut of your dress
Shows you're perky
The look in your eye
Is so fresh and so flirty
The tilt of your head
Your knees always spread
Your breath smells of sand
A banana
Half pealed
Tilts in your hand
I feel like I've know you
Since I was three
I love you
I love you
My stuffed monkey

Smooth Operationator

Sometimes love is short
Sometimes love is thin
Seems most of what I got
Is buried deep within'
At least until
After the surgery
When there will be more of me
That you can touch and feel
Instead of just a bite
I'm gonna be a meal

All About the Itch

Went down to see
My favorite whore
She's a little bit easy
But costs a little bit more
A couple days latter
I had a horrible itch
Doctor said be careful
Where I dig that ditch

Went up to see
My good-time slut
She don't ask no questions
When I'm under her gut
Come next morning
Got a horrible itch
Doctor said be careful
Where I scratch my itch

Went out to find
A girl I don't know
She's lookin' for company
If she's walking real slow
I like them a little strange
Cause I got that itch
Nothing beats a poor girl
When I'm feeling rich

BBQ You

Licking you
When you moan
Straight down
To the bone
They say I have a bloody thirst
And that's the part that really
hurts
Twisting me
Till my heart near bursts
So when I beat this wrap
Like that girl with my fist
I've already written up a list
Of people to get revenge upon
It's long
There'll be nothing left for the
hearse
The only question
Who to eat first

Bandito Magnifico

Loving you
Raccoon
With your pretty
Pretty paws
And under
A full moon
I fell like
A schoolgirl
Again
In the warm
Embrace
Of your jaws
Still come morning
We must part
You to your family
Me for some shots

Beached Without Lotion

Loving you
To grease the wheel
I'm the Orca
Not the seal
I'm devoted
My motion is geared
To gain
A promotion
Don't talk about morals
Cause I don't care
What do you mean
You don't work here
I can't believe
This happened
Again
Tell a friend

Not Stuck Enough

Loving you
Through
Two cans
Of glue
The only way
I will stay
After the nails
Fail
The rope
Broke
I escaped
The tape
If you want
This relationship to last
You better use something
That holds fast
Anything less
Than a whole lot more
And baby
I'm out the door

The Pill

Loving you
Enough to kill
Everyone
With a pill
It's bright yellow
Like the sun
You've given me religion
The only real
And truest one
That commands
Take the pill
Or else
All my love
And every thrill
Will all have been in vain
Turning love into pain
Though they're really
Both the same
Except for the refrain
And the way I pronounce
My god's name
When once I called you Candy
You're now Take-The-Pill
Which makes it salvation
And not just a kill

New Day Same You

Loving you
Day
After day
After day
After day after day
After day after day after day
After day after day
After day
After day
After day after day
After day after day after day
Oh please
Oh please
Won't you just go away

Low

Love is not art
It's craft
When you asked
If you butt looks good
I'm sorry I laughed
But Hey Zeus Christ
I've seen that thing
A hundred thousand times
But the faults not yours
And yours alone
Part of it is mine
I'm nearly empty
I've run so low
I need a shot
Of testosterone
Before this dog
Digs up a bone

Reduce Reuse and Cherish (Earth Day)

They told me
You were no good
Right from the start
But you still found
A rancid place
Inside my tiny heart
They said that you were rotten
Right down to the core
But that only made me hot
And want to love you more
But you cheated
Flagrantly
And you hit
Nails out
Angrily
Treating me like shit
For way too long
But I still say
About you
They are all wrong
You're worth at least
A little bit
You just need a better mentor
You're not just trash
So I brought you down
To the recycle center
And traded your evil brash
For a pocket full
Of sweet sweet cash

All Fours and Furry, Why You in a Hurry

The first time
I met you
I was taking a leak
You couldn't help
But take a peak
I could tell
By the way you held
Onto that limb
That you love nuts
All your life
Never enough
I said I've got
Just what you want
Gripping them tight
In my hand
Coaxing you down
Not giving a bite
Till all four limbs
Were on the ground
Then into your cheeks
I stuffed a hunk
You're awful cute
For a chipmunk

Bedtime Story

Loving you
Like a whore
That lies in the street
With no arms
And no legs
She bites at the feet
Of those walking by
Trying to meets
Someone who'll lift her
Up out of the street
Anyplace is better
Be it car trunk
Or trash
As rude as that sounds
Trash cures three kinds of rash
That she gets on her body
Where her meat
Meets the street
Which is where
I first met her
She was biting my feet
Breaking my heart
And piercing my meat
Oh God
Not a tongue
Not on my toes
I'd rather suck boogers
From a mucus clogged nose
It made me so sick
It made me go nuts
I kicked her twice in the head
And once in the gut
But she held on so tight
With such open glee
I didn't want to fight

I just wanted to flee
But she held on for dear life
So I dragged her
On her head
All the way home
And right into my bed
And loved her like no other
And that my son
Is how I first met your mother

The Big Bang

Loving you
No atmosphere
Sloppy mess
Floating everywhere
Should have never
Left the ship
Should have never
Chose to strip
Thank god I'm quick
Or I'd still be loaded
And we'd have wasted a trip
That ends in exploded

Beat Till Tender

Loving you
With a whip
Didn't work
It's not hot
It just hurt
The carrot
On the stick
Didn't do the trick
The hot sauce
Was a complete loss
And ether
Didn't do it either
Which is why
I bought the beaver
But the beaver broke
The goat choked
And the pigeons flew the coop
Taking animals
Out of the loop
They don't make love
They just make poop
And hitting you with my car
Only dented my fender
If pain don't work soon
I might have to be tender

The Roots of Love
(Arbor Day)

I love you
You're never afraid
To take a chance
I love you
You always
Have a stance
I respect you
Because you'd say anything
To anyone
But you never
Should have said that
Not about my mom
Not to me
Not today
Ruining our special lunch
Under the shade
Of our favorite tree
Celebrating
Something
You cared about
When you should have cared for
me
I supported your every crusade
Which is why
I dug a shallow grave
You didn't nurture me
But baby
You can feed
Our favorite tree

A Man to Meat Mamma

Loving you
Cause I'm high
And juicy
Goosey
Juicy
Add some flour
You got gravy
Lady
Wavy
Gravy
I'll throw up
Then baby maybe
I'll be able to get it up
And make you scream
Get up
Get up
You've fallen asleep
But all I hear
Is not a peep
Which makes it awkward
I've never met
Your parents before
And I'll do it
If ever
I can climb off the floor

Best Served Inside Out

You should know by now
I didn't only kiss her
I went out
And did it
I did it with your sister
But you drove me to it
And believe me
It wasn't easy
You don't have a sister
Just a willing brother
And it cost me every penny
That I got from my dear mother
To provide for her
In her old age
Want to talk about angry
I'm in a rage
That's why we flew to Bangkok
To saw your brother's thing off
Then some was tucked inside
And all he had to pay
For me making him that way
Was to give me the first ride
I was his first lay
And we liked it so much
We did it twice that day
So ha ha ha on you
You said it was over
Now I say that it's through
And you better believe
Me and Franketta
Are enjoying our life together
And unlike being with you
I don't even mind
The beard

Handles Make the Ride

I replaced
Your hair
With Astroturf
I know
It hurt
Your field was looking a little bare
It may not have bothered you
I don't care
If there's hair
On the girl
You can harvest
The pearl
So it's really not your call
Without grass
On the field
I won't play ball
And the handlebar mustache
Really adds a touch of class

May

Yesterday

Loving you
Till Tuesday
And though it's Wednesday
I'm not talking six days
Of nonstop sex
Where we huff
And we puff
And we get no rest
And I don't mean
I'll be such a great lay
I'll set you back an entire day
I only mean
That when I'm finished
You'll wish this day
Was one that isn't

Eye of the Storm

Loving you
Like a sun-dried tomato
And picked cucumber
Tornado
The only kind
I'd like to meet
Cause everything
That flies from you
Is good enough
To eat

Near as a Toe to an Ear

I can smell you
Everywhere I go
It's not perfume
It's just your toe
That I keep
In my sock
The left one
Although
It feels
Like a rock
I don't want it
To get lonesome
Like I used to be
Before the toe
Made me feel
Like you're near
At least that's what
I tell
Your ear

That Snow Child That's My Kid

Just so you know
You're the one
That suggested
We go out in the snow
And now that we're alone
I'm gonna give you
The bone
The only one
I got left
That ain't entirely froze
I know you've lost an arm
Your toes
And an ear
But I was surprised
Moved near
You started to crack
From your nose
To your rear
I had only one chance
For done
To be did
So I chipped you apart
And I aimed for a kid
And spent the rest
Of my life
On the note
Please defrost with care
There's a baby in there
Though only a tiny zygote

A Sandwich Just Isn't a Sandwich
(Cinco de Mayo)

I couldn't
Love you more
Unless you brought
A friend
So I could lay love
End to end
Love's not a knot
It's a chain
And always feels better
When you spread on
Some pain
A lesson I learned
Long ago
In a little town
In Mexico
While bread is good
A sandwich is better
So bring over Heather
And I'll provide the glaze
A rich creamy helping
Cinco de mayonnaise

You Look Soft Enough to Recline

Once upon a time
In a land of not to bright
I brought you home
Without a fight
And we spent
Such a night
Of ignorance
And pleasure
And since you didn't object
I bound you in leather
Inside a chair
And whispered softly
In your ear
Baby you're not really here
Which you seemed to believe
And I believe
You'll never leave
I feed you through a tube
And love you through a seem
Which would be mean
If you knew
If you could remember
That you existed
Anywhere
Ever

Ding Dong Little Gong

Ding
Ding
Ding
Went my
Ding-ding
Dong
Dong
Dong
Went my dong
It took
A whole lot of ringing
To finally
Bang that gong
When I heard you
Chiming
You didn't ring too long
The gong
Became a noodle
And I'm gone
Gone
Gone

Waiting on Another Ring

Loving you
You're a tree
And it seems to me
You've the body
Of a well-developed school girl
But despite all my talk
The rules say
Hands off
Cause as much as you've grown
And your body is happenin'
Truth be told
You're still just a sapling
And baby birch molesters
Have no protectors
In the jail yard
So I'll still buy you presents
Waiting for the day
When your white birch
Turn gray
And I get to start
Chopping away

Doing it English

Loving you
Over tea
Literally

Please Be Wet

Loving you
Cause I need
All the juice
I can suck
I'm thirsty
Dehydrated
And need every drop
So don't be surprise
If I want it
Again
And again
And again and again
They say that this drought
May never end

Looking the Other Way
Brought Me Around

Loving you
In the barn
Because that's
Where you live
Plowing all day
With still more to give
Resisting the urge
To loudly neigh
The others don't mind
My time in the hay
But I can't ever
Let them
Find out
That I'm neigh

Wanted

Wanted
Hepatitis C
Willing to pay
Upon delivered
It's the last one
I need
To complete my collection
From all over the world
I have every infection
It's been years
Since I've had
A normal erection
It's really not well
The way it hurts
How it swells
Hurts like hell
So swollen
It feels just like heaven
It's cracked and it sizzles
I need the pain
To rain
Now it's barely a drizzle
I need so much more
Which is what
I placed
This add for

Biting Wood

Loving you
Is so good
When I do it
With wood
That I carved with my teeth
And the toes on my feet
To look just like you
So you'll always be near
Is why I carved you my dear
Though your nose is too small
And your arms were bit off
You left legs are just balls
Cause the wood was too soft
It still looks just like you
If your head was all wrong
If you'd eaten a bomb
It's the best I could do
When I carve with my teeth
And the toes on my feet
Leaving me with wood
That would look just like you
If only it could

Yoke

Loving you
Chicken style
Lots of feathers
Lots of fluff
The cock will crow
I'll start to beg
Before it's over
We'll both agree
I really laid an egg

Upside of Being a Prick

Loving you
Though you could do
Much better
Keeping you down
So you'll stay
Forever
A touch of cruel
A helping of evil
I'm not a fool
I need you to bend
Not break
So when I'm nice
You'll mistake it for great
As long as you don't know
You're one of the best
You'll stay with me always
At least until death
Which could happen any day
If you listen to what your sisters
say
But they're just pissed
I tried to run them down
But I'm sorry
Sorry that I missed
They're fast for fat
But they're out of luck
I just bought
A bigger truck
No slipping by the bumper this
time
Then we'll be back
To being fine
Just as long
As you stay in line

Just Another Peanut Butter Mother
(Mother's Day)

I love you
My mother
With
Peanut butter
I love you
My mother
With cheese
I loved you
All your natural life
I loved you
Through the disease
Now I love
The parts I smoke
And the parts I freeze
You always said
While you're around
I'd never starve
So I carve
You so thin
I can see right through
It be a sin
To finish you
I just can't seem to do it
You were always so good to me
And now you are delicious
I miss you each and every day
There's no one to do the dishes

Either Hell or the Flue

Loving you
Even though
My nose
Needs a blow
My head
Throbs immensely
And though my blood flows
It does so densely
Loving you
Even though
My jaw just froze
I can't feel my toes
There's shit in my lungs
And what comes from my bum
Comes out on the run
Loving you
Though the fluid in my brain
Is massing
Gaining momentum
For one giant attack
One from which
I'm not coming back
But before I go
I'll spit in your eye
And bite through your tongue
Insuring you'll die
You'll be fried
You'll be done
This wasn't just an average date
You've always been
The one I hate
Since the day
You called my sister fat
Ran over my girlfriend
And molested my cat

I've hated you
From afar
For so long
Tonight
Nothing right
Kills
Something wrong

Good Times

Loving you
With a Twinkie
Dipped into
A brown martini
Frozen with some nitrogen
Now's your chance
You'd better run
The snakes are coming soon
Followed by a hot glass shower
And then a rancid coon
I'll show you how a second
Can feel just like an hour
We may die
Before we're done
But baby
Ain't we having fun

It's Thicker

Loving you
Through a hole
In the wall
Of the peep show booth
I don't know who you are
But you're missing a tooth
And you must be on your knees
The hole is so low
Only a midget could stand
There's no way to know
If you're really a man
But if I think too much
I feel whiskery lips
And hair on your hand
So I know you're Italian
And though I don't know where
you've been
I close my eyes
And it seems
You must be
The girl of my dreams
So when I cum
When I'm finally done
I won't be ashamed
Of what I just banged
Through a hole in the wall
If you saw what I imagined
You wouldn't blame me at all
Thanks to Mrs. Butterworth

Heads You Win

Loving you
My mamma
Told me to
Your family has money
I was an accident
My skins golden honey
Your nose is bent
I'm hung like a horse
You're beard is coarse
Women love me
You're from money
We will have a marriage
And distress
We will have children
And unrest
Our marital bed will stink
Of your feet
And my mistress
But don't worry
Of each other
We'll never be free
We're just two sides
Of the same disease

Long Way Down

Some men
Love
Six inches
I love
Past six feet
The only way
To keep love fresh
Is to keep on digging deep

Well Hung Up

Loving you
From 2,000 miles away
Is for the best
I never know what to say
I usually run
If I hear the word breast
But since you do all the talking
I feel like I can stay
And I can't see you anyway
Unless I close my eyes
Real tight
Still try as I might
I can't get it up
It ain't worth the fight
I should hang up
I know
I know
I still have to pay
But it will only cost more
If I stay on all day
When all I'm getting
Is an ache in my head
Not that one
That one's still dead
Of course it isn't you
But it is
At the rate I'm going
I'll never have kids
If I look at a girl
My dick tries to hide
If I talk to one
It hitches a ride
No
I've never tried
Hitting it

With a bone
I think it's time
I hung up the phone
For the sake of my dick
Click

Too Good to be Stepped On

Loving you
One line
At a time
Chopping you up
Extra fine
I'll get halfway through your
head
So full of love
I end up dead
Who knew
I'd overdose on you
Who knew
You'd be so pure
Loving you
Has no cure
If I had it to do all over again
I'd only do you faster
Snorting more desire
Getting higher
Before I expire
Cause it's hard to find a dealer
When you're dead
You can't take love with you
My advice
Fill your head

Taking You Home

Loving you
Cause I'm bored
I don't care anymore
I've turned you down
A thousand ways
A new rejection every day
The only thing worse
Than a night with
A misshapen, club-footed, rash
blotched, gassy, pock marked,
vein marred, chicken scarred,
horse headed, herd trampled,
meteor impacted, boring as a
giant pan of half burnt nasty old
you
Is finding a way to avoid it
You can't be shaken
Won't take the clue
So I'm gonna take you home
And be rid of you
By giving you the bone
Deep down and nasty
And I'm not saying hot
I'll piss in your bed
And fart on your head
Put my dick in your ear
Slip your lips in my armpit
Your nose in my rear
I'll swear I'm your grandpa
The kinky old fellow
Vomit in your crotch
Blow my nose on your pillow
I'll wear your hair
Like a thong
Bending you over

All wrong
Instead of my dick
I'll use a brick
And a brush
All designed
To end this crush
Without so much as a moan
Then I'll shit on the carpet
Before I head home
Maybe that will teach you
To leave me alone

Killer Babe

Loving you
As blood runs down my nose
Loving you
Though it cost
Eight of my toes
Loving you
Though the yearning
Near took off my head
Punctured my heart
Filled my lungs
Full of red
Loving you
Though the holes in my chest
Run all the way through
The romantic
In me
Loves the killer
In you
Though not for much longer
I fear that your love
Has left me
A goner

Good Till the Last Toe

You're my favorite girl
In the whole
Wide
World
My love is true
I'll always be loyal
I kept you in the freezer
So that you won't spoil
But the powers
Been out
For 48 hours
And rot
Is taking
Your meat
Your head went bad
Yesterday
From too much friction heat
But I'm gonna kept it anyway
I'll just have to preserve you
Another way
But all your bits
Needed care
And I feel bad I wasn't there
In time
Most of you went this morning
I was with you just last night
I should have bought ice
I had plenty of warning
All that good
Firm
Frozen meat
And all I could save
Is your dirty old feet
And feet are no good
For kissin'

But with the right socks
You're still a fox
And I get right down
To lickin'

Thumbs Up

Loving
My thumb
Whom I've knows
For years
My friend
My thumb
The one
Who cares
The only one I trust
Anything bad
That comes
Between us
Can be washed away
With a mild
Detergent
Our love
Is calm
And sweet
And never feels urgent
We have plenty of time
We'll be together
Forever
That thumb is mine
Unless it pisses me off
Then it's the old
Chop and toss

Does That Finger Go All the Way Up to the Nail

How cold
Must you be
Before I freeze
How far
Must I sink
Before I'm on my knees
How much pain can I take
Before I finally break
My life was once light
I felt like a feather
Now I'm bound
To be lashed
With a cattail of leather
These are the things
That will keep us
Together

Who Da Bomb Now

If the shelter is a rockin'
Don't come a knockin'
I'm loving you
Cause the bombs
Are a droppin'
We've got fifteen minutes
Left to live
And baby
I still got more to give
And I ain't goin'
Till this loads a blowin'

Who Would Jesus Do

Loving you
Cause
God damn it
That's what Jesus
Would do
After getting drunk
At the football rally
And finding you alone
In that dark alley
You called me
Someone else's name
We're having a baby
All the same
So what would Jesus do
I gotta think
He'd marry you
As soon
As his stint
In jail
Is through

Mo Money

Loving you
You're the first one
The first one I could find
I have only
Half an hour
And that's not much time
I've got only
Forty dollars
And that's not a lot of money
For a girl I can't stand
But keeps calling honey
Propped against
A trash can
Feeling kinda funny
The wind blowing
Across my bare ass
As I pump away
And you count the cash
I only wish
You were

More
Attractive
Less
Drug addicted
Of
Legal age
Possessing
More limbs
Containing
Some teeth
Nearly
Coherent
Somewhat
Clean
You're so loose
I barely make a dent
At least I still have time for lunch
And money for the rent
God
I gotta start
Make more
So I can afford
A better whore

June

Taking the Time

Loving you
From head
To toe
So slow
That when I get back
From your toes
To your head
You're dead

Fishy

Loving you
With a roll
Of coins
From the bank
And some leftover parts
From an old fishy tank
It's a kind of love
You can't take for long
And before you can count them
My quarters are gone
And what was a pump
Now fits like a thong
And I can tell from your face
You think something's wrong
But I assure you
If I didn't know
What I was doing
I'd still have the fish
Now wouldn't I

Full Moon

Loving you
With cheese
From the moon
Make room
I got a shuttle's worth
More than you
Could ever stand
Now we'll see
Who's not a man

You're Giving Me the Runs

Loving you
When you didn't expect it
And now you're expecting
Destroying many years
Of damn fine neglecting
I hate to think
I'll have to start
Paying attention
Because of one
Misguided erection
I feel like I won
The wrong election
I wasn't even running
But I'm running now
And I not gonna stop
Till I'm out of this town

Free Delivery Within

Loving you
Because I have nothing
Nothing else to do
A punishment
For all I've done
I've done it all
All on the run
And baby
It was always fun
But those days are over
Done
No more
Now sex is all
They can't test me for
I'll be shot
If I set foot
Outside of my door
They'll slice off my head
And rip out my liver
Praise god
For a whore
Kind enough
To deliver

The Old Breeze Blows

Shooting air
Not quit there
Pulling you
Not quit near
Is a little more
Than I can bear
If only you
Would disappear
And I could be a younger man
Free of the cold
Exchanging blanks
For quit a load

Your Sign is Stop

Loving you
With too much force
Riding you
Like I'm breaking
A horse
Nearly killed you
Or course
I didn't see
The sign
In time
I couldn't hear
The hurt
I should have
Kept my eyes open
When I kicked you
With my boot
Never depend
On safety words
When you dominate
A mute

Talk to the Little Man

Don't mean
To be rude
I don't care
What you think
I don't love you at all
And you're loves for my dink
If you must speak
Please direct it
To him
His stature is stout
His understanding
Slim
It's obvious
You two
Have a lot in common
And discretion dictates
I should leave you two alone
But hold onto your underwear
It's time I go home
And though
You both
Are made mostly of bone
It's still gonna hurt
When I'm in bed alone

Painful Little Secret

Loving you
You don't know
You're my foe
I'll get you all hot
Then knock out your teeth
Grabbing you throat
Like a fist full of meat
Slapping you
To and fro
Tearing
Out your hair
Pulling you near
To scream
In your ear
Telling
The things
I'm going to do
Some of which
Will hurt
And some of which
Will hurt a lot
And when we're through
And you're limping away
You'll be glad
For what you got

Your Best Sides Your Shoes

Loving you
Was arranged
When we were just two
Most likely by people
Who hadn't a clue
Even back then
You behaved like a bitch
My momma said
Shut up boy
You're lucky
She's rich
And you grew
To be
A stone cold fox
But I'd be better off
With a bride
From a box
With some assembly required
Nothing about you
Lights my desire
Maybe if we turned that mouth
off
And I forgot
We ever met
Maybe if you soaped up
And got really wet
Then I'd know
How deep
Shallow goes
There's nothing I like better
Than a girl with a hose
To turn your crab grass
Into a rose
A beautiful flower
I'd immediately cut

Just to watch die
When the water stops
And you go back to dry
All you'll be is a bitch
Better to pull the flower
And leave you in the ditch

You'll Get Yours

Scream all you want
It doesn't make sense
Everyone loves
An electric fence
Holler if you have to
Turn all shades of purple
I know for a fact
The whole world loves gerbils
And you're not fooling me
By looking so sad
I know people
Who'd kill
For the ball kind of gag
Ah
Now that's the look
I expected to see
Evil glaring back at me
And all it took
Was a little burn
And me telling you
It's now your turn

Stung Sting Stain

There's a bug
That I love
And it hovers just above
Me
In my
Pajamas
I don't know
What words to say
I'm just hoping
It will stay
So for now
I'm careful
Of my
Manners
But soon will come a night
When I'll be brave
And invite
It
To cover
All the bases
I'll stroke its little wings
And when I coax it
It will sting
Me
In all
The right places

Toaster Oven Lovin'

That's my mother
She's got some butter
She calls me toast
Instead of her lover
I don't mean to boast
I ain't like the others
She loves me the most
Even more than her brothers
And they don't love me at all
One I call Turkey
The other one's Paul
There's only one thing to do
I eat them up
Turning them into poo
But don't tell my mother
I ate her brothers
Or she will want some too

Wave High Before Wiping
(Flag Day)

They said
It was Flag Day
But I misunderstood
They said
It was patriotic
I vowed to do what I could
They said
It's for America
I promised to help
All those in need
But everyone
That needed me
Seemed to want me
On my knees
I think this holiday
Will be my last
I most likely die
From the pain
That's screaming out
My ass

Stormy Weather

When the wind blows
And you don't
I get angry
Baby
When the thunder crashes
Like a rock and roll band
After the groupies
Have all gone home
And I'm making love
To my hand
It makes me crazy
Baby
You should have put out
Before this storm came about
Before the lightning
Before the rain
The blue balls
The pain
That drove me
Insane
And that's my plea
And if one man
On the jury
Can relate
Or even
To agree
Tomorrow
I'll be free

Bottled Fresh

Loving you
With a cork
To keep you fresh
Until tomorrow
Today
I expect company
And I don't want them
To see me this way
I've had too much already
Still I don't want them
To have any
So I'm putting you
Up
On the shelf
Till I can finish you
Off myself

Have Meatball Will Roll

On top of old Smokey
A five-dollar whore
When for the first time
I can't do it no more
It's not just the smell
And it's not just the age
It's really the fact that
I just got a raise
And think it's time
To use my shiny new dime
For an up-grade
I pretty sure
For five dollars more
I can get
Twice the whore

Double D Dad
(Father's Day)

There's a man
I love
And that ain't bad
His name is Gus
But I call him dad
He's the best father
I ever had
He loves me
He helps me
He makes sure
I'm all right
He listens to my problems
He reads to me at night
I haven't always had him
It hasn't been that long
Still he made me a man
Taught me right from wrong
And knows everything about
women
From when
He was
My mom

A Little Less Than You Know

Loving you
In a way
That is short
Short of love
Short of passion
Short of cash
Shooting off like a gun
The only thing faster
Is how quick I run
Too fast to catch
All you will see
Of me
Is my ass
As I vanish without a trace
Along with my cash
You'll never remember my face
I wasn't a good time
I'm bound to be
A blip in your mind
Such a small man
A pimp can't find

With or Without Bumpers

I made a statue
Of you
Out of spam
They say it's the meat
That tastes most like man
Or woman
In your case
A pretty dress
Covered in lace
A bowling ball
For your face
We can dance
The night away
Our bodies meshed
Like so much clay
As we bowl another frame
You're still the one
With the bigger brain

The Short and the Short of It
(Summer Solstice)

Loving you
On the longest day
With the shortest part
Of me
Sorry
But
That's what you get for free
Little tiny skinny me
Maybe
I should have been saved
For a shorter day
Or you could have saved some
cash
For someone
With a mighty stash
We got nothing
But time
The suns barely up
And so am I
Nothing left to do
But cry
Which I'm gonna
Go ahead
And consider
Foreplay
It's the only way
We'll get through
This day

What a Boar

I always said I wouldn't
But I did
Loving you for money
Even though
You're a pig
Rough
With tusks
That I fear
May scar
Never take money
From pigs
In a bar
Never after
Seven drinks
Pigs want their monies worth
And though they have small
dinks
Their hooves really hurt
I never meant to go this far
Now I can't go back
To another bar

Wham Bam Hit It Again

It pains me
When I think
How we met
Without so many drinks
At the bar
I'm willing to bet
We wouldn't be together
Not without my car
And it's quick acceleration
I plowed you down
You said 'Hi I'm Heather'
Since that day
We've been together
Now people can say
Whatever they wish
But I'm never going to dump her
She's and integral part
Of my front bumper

Not for the Squeamish

Loving you
With a stick
Covered in beer
God that's sick
I'm out of here

Never Say Ever

They say
You regret
Most
The things
You never do
And baby
I never
Have ever
Done you
Halleluiah!
Halleluiah!
Halla Halla Lu!
While I don't know
What you have
I know the things you do
I know the things you did
God I couldn't be happier
That is not my kid
You're the worst I ever met
The best I'll never do
And baby
Believe
I won't regret you

Next Time Leave the
Batteries at Home

Loving you
In a way
That embarrassed
Us both
It seemed like
A good plan
When I bought
The remote
I thought it would work
When I programmed the goat
But all we got was shame
What should have been
The greatest sex of our lives
Was
And I'll love you
Forever
Because
Accidentally
Broadcasting
Bestiality
Means
No one wants
To be
With you or me

More Every Morning

The new car smell
Has gone out
Of your britches
You're stained
And you're torn
With algae bloom itches
I'd like to call you
In for breakfast
But you don't fit
Through the door
Oh baby
What are we
Fighting for
No man
Could ever
Ask for more

No Room For Seconds

Loving you
Double time
On account
Of the line
I don't wish
To be rude
Two by two
Four by four
The line is still
Right out the door
And some
Are coming back
For more
In line
A second time
Sure they'll be fine
Ready again
When they get to the front
The ones that can't wait
Are having at my behind
Which is why
I'm loving you
Double time

Not a Log Big Enough for This Fire

Loving you
With a torch
To keep the bad things away
Day after
Day after
Day after day
The fire inside me
And out of you
Grows
Overwhelming my heart
And turning you black
I knew from first light
They'd be no turning back
As I singed your toes
And blacked your head
I'm changing
My favorite
Color
To red
Just like the rose
That silently
Bled
And as I pass
The torch by again
I know
I'm no slave
To desire
Bad things
Must be kept
Away
With fire

An Itch is not an Itch

Loving you
For two bucks
And that includes tip
Which is more than you're worth
Turning tricks
When you're sick
But an itch
Is an itch
Is an itch
Is an itch
And though the two dollars
Was meant for hot scratching
My tender places
Are clearly reacting
Giving birth to new itching
And the wrong kind of scratching
Which will lead to infection
And some non-stop crapping
Giving me time to reflect
That when I get an itch
And need a deep sip
I should always be careful
And not over tip

July

Love Comes With Age

I'm too old
Too love you
Without a jump start
Left on my own
I'm lucky to fart
It's been so damn long
I'm not sure I can
So let's concentrate
On making it stand
Pass the rubber bands
That keep up my socks
Add some glue
Lots of tape
And a few shards of glass
And I'll be ready
To hit that sweet little ass
With the right medications
I'm told never to mix
Even though
Doctors know
How they jump-start my dick
That's just like him
He's a real nasty prick
That banged my wife
In my bed
Before letting me know
She was finally dead
So let's get it on
I think I can take it
Though if I don't make it
And I die tonight

Departing this land
You'll find my wallet
Left on the night stand

Not Fade Away

Loving you
With lots of lotion
Because I chafe
And I blister
From your gutter ball motion
But I can't just rub it all over the
place
I gotta make sure
I don't cover your face
So carefully drawn
In just the right place
A love so pure
I'll never erase
When we do it
It looks like you're choking
Then comes the burning
Then comes the smoking
And if the lotion
Rides as high as your ear
You start to smear
Which is why lotions control's
So important
My dear

Run of the Mill, Sugar

Loving you
Till I've had my fill
Then it's off
You go
To the mill
Processing you
For financial gain
Into a lovely
Lovers
Grain
But before
You go to the store
I'll have to have you
At least once more
Right there
On the milling floor
Before I sift you
Into
A you-size sack
Carrying you
To the machine out back
Processing you
Into the sweetest snack
That before I sell
I again have at
There's more to you
Than just fine milling
You're not a dessert
Without cream filling

High We Shall Fly
(4th of July)

Loving you
With a rocket
Pointed toward the sky
The orchestra sounds
Flags held high
You ate so much BBQ
I feared
You wouldn't get off
So I sheered
Some parts of you off
To get you aloft
Lighting you up
Like a flair
Towards the crowd
With wild cheers
As you explode
High in the air
The colors so bright
The night so clear
I could nearly cry
God I love
The 4th of July

Like a Locomotive

Loving you
On the wrong side
Of the track
The side where
The train is coming
And so am I
I don't know
Which will
Hit you first
The train
Or I
I'm kinda hopping
It's a tie
What a way
To fuck and die

Next Stop is Get the Hell Off

Loving you
Like a locomotive
I only go one way
And you're gonna
Have to pay
For every minute
Of the ride
That you decide
To stay
And when
Your ride
Is through
I'll pick up
Someone new
Going on
Without you

Junky

Loving you
Like there's pleasure receptors
All over my brain
Calling your name
The voices get loud
I'm going insane
I need to be with you
I don't care the cost
I need you to be here
For when you're not near
I begin to tear
Around the house
Searching
For anything
That may contain
A trace of you
A tiny piece
Some residue
To help me get through
To quiet the screams
Taking over my mind
Line by line
A dime at a time
Though every day I swear
We are through
It don't last long
I'm addicted to you

Nothing Legal

Loving you
You're my nanny
And you're illegal
So what you gonna do 'bout it
Huh
What you gonna do
Just be thankful I'm still paying
you
There's always the hole
Where my old nannies stay
So dark
And so damp
Can't tell nights
From the day
Or your head
From your feet
And all you can eat
Is old nanny meat
So don't mess
With me
You'd regret it
If you did
And so would I
You're so good with the kids

Love Means Never Cross the Streams

You said
It's not an Adam's apple
It's an Eve
You said
It's not a wiener
It's a weave
You said it
All so sexily
I didn't get up
And leave
While you gripped me
So strongly
There are bruises
On my knee
I said I like
To be the man
You said
That I must understand
That you stand
When you pee
I said
That doesn't bother me
For a long
Long time
I've been really lonely
Just please
Don't tell my mommy
She'd be shocked
I turned out this way
She away thought
I'd end up gay

Not Loving You at All

I'd love you
In the back room
Where you sleep
And boy
Let me tell you
You sleep deep
It would be so easy
For me to sneak
A little further
Then I usually do
Taking more than a peek
Straddling you
But that's a place
I'll never go
Not cause
I care
For you
Deeply so
Or fear
You will wake
I'm just not
Good enough
Man enough
Don't have enough
So small
I'd barely
Be raping you
At all

One of Us has to Get Pretty Quick

Believe me
I understand
And I know
We could be more proactive
There are thing that we could do
To make you more attractive
Make a better looking you
And I'm not refusing to pay
For the implants
Just to be mean
You are truly the ugliest
I've ever seen
But that's what keeps you
faithful
It's hard to cheat
When no one wants you
And I ain't exactly pretty myself
Unless I get some implants too
In which case
I don't need you
What a thought
What a thing to do
I'll get the implants for myself
And you can be ugly
With somebody else

Octopus, Octopus, Octopus, You

Loving you
In my dreams
Where I am young and mighty
And it seems
You are unusually multi-ethnic
An octopus of women
That looks
Nothing like you
Acts
Nothing like you
Doesn't whine
And aren't always telling me
What to do
But I'm sure
That they're you
Who else would I do
In my dreams
Loving you

Out Out Damn Hog

Loving you
I'm an outlaw
On the back
Of my hog
His name is Wilber
He likes apples
He doesn't know
He's a pig
He thinks
He's a car
If you'll believe
We're in his backseat
I'm sure that I'll get far

It Came Up Twice

Video clip
Spit
Hawk
Vomit
Roll over
Buffer
Buffer
Approve
Snork
Hawk
Velvet
Strain
Rear
Tuna fish
In the ear
Love it
Love it
Vomit

Delivery Refused

Loving you
Like Chinese food
I'll be hungry again
To damn soon
Forget the French
Give me Lo Mein
Not Karma Sutra
But Kung Pow
I want you delivered
Delivered right now
But alas it cannot be
You're almost pure
MSG

Till Death or Tuesday

Loving you
For 46 million reasons and
change
You won't last
Another season
You're always in pain
Doctors say you have cancer
But I think it's the mange
Doctors say your mind is
slipping
But I say you're deranged
But you still have needs
Or at least desires
You bodies cold
But you think you're on fire
To quench that thirst
I fill your cup
And I'm so damn good
There's no prenup
I've broken your will
Laid claim to your assets
I'm built to kill
With all the right facets
And now that we've
Said I do
I give it to you
With so much heat
You're burning up
From your head
To your feet
Till all that's left
Is your false teeth

Loving You With Milk

Loving you
Lack luster
So fat
Can't muster
My belly
Your belly
Can't get to you
What do we do
Oh what do we do
The once familiar
No longer fits
Maybe we need
To research a bit
We could look up
Chubby nookie
Or turn on the TV
And eat some more cookies
I see
We agree
No need to fight
A bucket of cookies
And we'll have a nice night

Other Family's Man

I never met
A child
I didn't invite
Into my van
That's where
I keep the candy
If you understand
There they eat
Everything
They can pull near
As I whisper
Soft but clear
Into their little ear
I love you
I love you
I love you
It's true
Which is why
The government
Monitors
All that I do

Being Me Being You

I love you
In the morning
I love you in the day
But when I love you the best
Is when you've gone away
Then I get to really be me
And then I get
To really be you
You'd hardly believe
The dirty things that you do
When you're gone
Several of them
Are morally wrong
And some of them illegal
If you were here
You'd understand
Why I bought the beagle
Or maybe you wouldn't
Cause you're not me
Though I'd like you to be
But we'll talk about that
When you get back
Right now
I got you to be
Doing me

The Noodles You Don't Want to Know

Loving you
With the biggest
Part of my brain
Giving you the best
Of what still remains
Everything I have left
That's not been removed
Where there should be thick
noodles
You'll only find only stew
And what's left
Sails upon
The black waters
Of my brain
Trapped endlessly
In a warped hurricane
The poorly manned ship
Tossed to and fro
Torn down to shit
But I don't complain
What I was
Wasn't right
Not right in the brain
They scooped out the sick
And left only sane
If you'd ever met
That part of my mind
That called it self
Freddy the Cow
You'd be dead now

Rows On the Skid

Loving you
Even though
You're on skid row
Sentenced to die
For horrible crimes
And though I'm naive
I don't really mind
You're my piece of pie
I'll write everyday
Till the day that you die
And when you're dead
I'll dream
Of naughty things
Alone in my bed
Rereading letters
So many times read
Telling anyone who'll listen
The profound things you said
And how
At heart
You were deep
And kind
And yes while it's true
You committed the crime
It wasn't your fault
You were raised all wrong
They'd broken your will
Growing up in Hoboken
You had no choice but kill
It wasn't your fault
Society let it
Or maybe I'm really
That fat and pathetic

More or Less

I said
I love you
Not that I
Expect you
To be faithful
But I would like
A discount
I'm not looking to cuddle
I don't need more hugs
And I don't care
That you do
A shit load of drugs
And I'm not worried
About the women
You call honey
Just charge them more
And me less money
And I swear
I'll never ask for anything again
I won't even mention the other
men
I'm not even asking
You give me your best
I only ask
That you charge me less

The Bigger the Cushion

Loving you
Every time
You are gone
Well
Not so much you
As I'm loving
Your thong
Wrapped around your pillow
I'm just that kind of fellow
And I want you to know
It's not wrong
This ain't about morality
Cause I do the same damn thing
When you're here
At least twice a day
Anyway

Oysters on My the Better Half

Loving you
Thanks to oysters
Nearly a ton
It took that much
To hold you down
Now we're having fun
Two fine hours
Or shucking shells
Then what the hell
Dinner for everyone
And you'll feel better about us
And better about me
Unless you get hepatitis C

Tongue and Laces

Loving you
Is killing me
And it's destroying
My knees
From the time that I spend
As the most lowly of men
Loving you
And your shoe
Is the best I can do
On the dollar or two
I didn't give you
And it's true
I'd do it again
Now that your shoe
Has become my best friend
I just hate to think
Where this might end

Revved Up and Off

Loving you
Left of center
Which I apologize for
I can't see
Very much
Very well
Anymore
I'm not even sure
How I got this far
But there's a damn good chance
In the morning light
You'll turn out
To be
My car

The Machine will Close the Deal

Loving you
From a distance
Of 200 yards
You say that's too easy
The law says it's too hard
That I'm just sleazy
Not really a threat
Which just goes to prove
They don't know me yet
Not like you
So knowledgeable
Of the things I can do
Of what I'm capable
But don't worry
I don't think you're rape-able
I think you're a doll
I don't want your body
I want it all
And there's more
Than one way
To skin a cat
I don't have to be
Right where you're at
Now that I've made
A mechanical man
That will act like I act
And be like I am
But not so scary
More like your type
A man you would marry
And whom I may live
Vicariously through
The only thing worse
Is not being with you

No Lotion for That

You are my sunshine
The kind that burns
From over exposure
Leaving blisters all over
Fractures
And cracking
I have no resistance
To all that you're lacking
You are the sweet light
Of an opulent moon
That uses its gravity
To bring a monsoon
Leaving me wrinkled
And cold
From the long
Flooded night
Full of incoming waves
That I can't escape
Till the grave
Safe
Buried deep in the ground
The cold earth
Feels warm on my face
Compared to a lifetime
In your embrace

Soul Love

Loving you
Everyday
That my wife is away
Loving you
Everyday
Though I'm not really gay
You have moles
On your holes
And real stinky toes
Your teeth are black
You smell like bad egg
And there's something wrong
With the shape of your head
Loving you
Everyday
Because I have nothing better to
do
And to find
Anything else
I'd have to leave my house
So while my wife is away
I'll love you everyday
And the other foot too

Parental Approval

Loving you
With a rage
I didn't know
I had
I'm sorry
I don't know why
I was calling you dad
I swear
The bruises
Ain't really that bad
I swear this kind of thing
Happens
Hardly ever
And I swear
It won't happen
Not again
Never
Unless that's what you're into
What's convention
To dictate
The things that we do
The way we act
What is right
What is wrong
What is good
What is bad
So if you want
Try calling me dad
But I hope
It won't be long
Before you're comfy enough
To start calling me mom

Pushing You Pushing Back

Loving you
By the edge
Of a cliff
Getting off
Looking over
The precipice
I know you're
Not really
Into this
But fear
Is making
You react
While passions
Something
That you lack
At least
This way
You're pushing
Back

August

Keep Your Eye on My Lust

Hypnotized
To love your eyes
Mesmerized
By flashing thighs
I only wanted
To quit smoking
Now all I want
Is to be your token
Whore
I paid a lot
You paid more
Now I'm breaking
Down your door
And you don't care
Not for me
Swearing
I was never there
Always booming with laughter
And the worst part is
I need
A cigarette after

Rock's Off

You threw me a rope
With a rock wrapped around
Always finding new ways
Of letting me down
I won't cry for help
I just assume drown
Then be pulled back to shore
So you can try
To kill me some more
Like you love to do
I think it's the thing
That defines me
And you
The way
You try
To make me die
Every day
And the fact
That I keep coming back
Even though
I don't get laid
Even though
I feel only pain
Am bound to die any day
What the hell
Am I trying to say

Can't Stand the Weight

Loving you
On the moon
With a bang
And a boom
Can't hold on
Drifting away
Damn you
Damn you
Low gravity

How I was Brought Up

Loving you
Like my brother
Makes love
To my mother
With eyes closed
And toes clenched
The things I do
To pay the rent
On my eye lids
I run a movie
Of all the girls
That wouldn't do me
I line then up
In a row
And that's as far as I get
Before I blow
Which is probably why
You never leave a tip
Come back soon
Ya' here

Personal Piper

Loving you
Is easy
Since you had the stroke
And you're short term memory
is gone
Cause old lady
Or should I call you baby
I'm never long
And we're always alone
I take care of the home
I'm more like
The pied piper
Than a rat
The kind that has at ya
Every time I change your diaper
When I'm staring at that flesh
Powder fresh
God
I'm just a man
Which I'm sure your family
Would understand
I'm a fish
Attracted to the bait
God I hope
This isn't on tape

Family Loves Pink Places

Loving you
You're the right color
The right color
At least
To take home
To mother
Don't get me wrong
My mother's a saint
You should feel relieved
This explains all the paint
It's not a change
In your pigment
You don't need a doctor
It's barely malignant
Now aren't you glad
It's not what you think
It's the best I can do
My mom only likes pink
And if all works out
You can get a tattooe
Your whole body inked
My mom will approve
And she'll let us be joined
Then we'll put her away
In a home
And enjoy some time
Pink
Rich
And alone

Sneaking In When the Parties Over

There's a party
In my pants
And I'm not invited
I can hear the music playing
But I'm not allowed to dance
If I get to close
They chase me away
Throwing glass
And insults
Yelling that
I'm gay
Which is very confusing
Not that I'm confused
Not like that
But it keeps me
From trying
The back door
I'm so off track
This has never happened before
And is not
What I expected
When first
I found
What was
Erected

Red Dress Debacle

Loving you
In a dress
That you don't know of yet
You think
I'm a real average guy
Just like all the rest
But really I'm a mess
And later on
When you're surprised
I hope the cries
Are that of joy
I'm your girl
I'm your boy
Please don 't throw a fit
Either way
One things for sure
Someone's getting hit

Beyond and Beyond

Loving you
Through a hole
I made
In your grave
Was your final wish
And I'm just the
Guy to dig that ditch
Which is what
I'll need to do
Cause even with the hole
I'm way too small
My dicks not a mole
A badger or worm
It will be a long night
Before you get your last turn

Bewitched Bewhored

Loving you
You demand it
Loving you
I don't like it a bit
Loving you
Anywhere
You want
Anytime
You desire
If I don't
You'll let them
Set me on fire
A witch
Is a witch
Is a witch
Is a witch
Unless she's willing to dig that
ditch
Then a whore
Is a whore
Is a whore
Is a whore
To set one on fire
Means she's aching for more
And a whore don't get burnt
Less she got the disease
Till then
I'll do whatever you please
It takes time
To cast
The proper spell
But by the end of this week
You'll wake up in hell

When You Were Ten

Loving you
Once again
Like you're only ten
And I still own the van
Loving you
Like you aren't
Really a man
Like I'm not in jail
Imagine me
Piece of tail
Cause I'm small
Here
But bigger than you
When
You were just ten
Least that's what I pretend
When my face meets my pillow
And my bed starts to squeak
It's a screech
Then a holler
Forced out by male caller
That comes every night
So I no longer fight
Making every bad thing I've
done
Feel really not right

Ode to Love

I can't
Even describe
How much
I love you
The end

The Wrong Side of Your Hill

Loving you
Is an uphill battle
Now that I'm over the hill
My bones all rattle
I wouldn't get up
If it weren't for the energy pills
I have an intravenous
Viagra drip
But as my breath
Fades
From your lips
And into oblivion
You do slip
Forgetting me
Before I go
I'm just someone
You don't know
Cause when you're an old timer
Most of your lovers
Have Alzheimer's

Stuck to Shoe

Loving you
Like I'm gum
I am stuck
To your shoe
To your shoe
I am stuck
Like gum
Loving you

Romance Blackout

Loving you
Cause the cable
Is out
And I
Don't know
What to do
When
That happens

Meat My Own

Loving you
With a dick
I don't own
It's not borrowed
And it's not on loan
I found it in the street
In the gutter
Under a car
Cause baby
Though I love you
And you're my shining star
A star can be filthy
Red giant infected
From all the diseases
That you've gone and collected
You're the dirtiest thing
I've ever met
The best part of your body
Smells worse than my feet
And as long as I live
You won't touch my meat

Wrong Hole

There's a hole in your wall
But I drilled it too high
You are not that tall
I can't see you at all
There's a hole in your floor
Leaving me wanting more
Some knee or some thigh
Something sweet
Really I'm not into feet
There's a hole in your roof
I'll be the first to admit
That one was a goof
I'd have be
A deranged fanatic
To want to peer into your attic
In search of something more
appealing
I drilled
Into your ceiling
But that's where all the hot
steams goes
It burns my eyes
And fills my nose
I'm narrowing down
I'm honing in
Of the parts of you
Made just for sin
What I want to see
In your precious flower
So I drilled a hole
Facing your shower
I put it above the bathroom sink
Now I know
You have a dink

Nothing Up Till I'm Down

I love you
Honestly
No really
I swear
Normally
The thought of you
Is more than my pants
Can bear
It's not you
It's just bad luck
When I got the pills
I took too much
And now I can't feel my face
Hell
I can't feel any place
And the way your eyes merge
And your lips disappear
As we draw near
Is really freaking me out right
now
But hold the thought
I'd love some love
As soon as I come down

She'll be Cumming Round My Mountain

Loving you
And the horse
You rode in on
I'm a sucker for twins
Don't look at me like that
And it ain't like you're kin
It ain't so wrong
Once you have on
Leather thongs
Even better after some wine
And some hay
Just enough
To perk us up
Before we start to play
And I'll give you my personal
Guarantee
That after they've been properly
bedded
It's not just the cowgirl
Who'll be walking bow-legged

A Bill Called Freedom

You can call me honey
If you got the money
In front of immigration
Keeping you from deportation
Or it's Cuba for the Cuban
And Haiti for the Haitian
But don't get confused
This ain't no vacation
Touch me and I'll kill you
For everything else
I'll bill you

Stuck to You

Loving you
My beautiful glue
As full as the moon
Tonight
An opulent glow
Reflects the street light
I couldn't ask
For anything more
Next to you
Paint's just a whore
Always spraying
In my face
Colors dripping
Across my head
Coating me in disgrace
But not you
You never make me look a fool
Any wonder
That in love we fell
Although I don't breath very
well
My nose
A swollen
Burning hell
While my brain is in heaven
Light and fluffy
Like dough that's been leaven
But with all the stuffin'
And the huffin'
I won't last long
But I'm not gonna call this
wrong
And I ain't giving up
We're bound together
Call it luck

For tight together
We are stuck

Love can be Ugly Up Close

Loving you
May seem rash
Since I've only
Seen your ass
But if you have the face
To match
Then this may be love
But if you're ugg
I'll close my eyes
And concentrate
Upon those thighs
I'm not so dumb
I'm kinda smart
I know ugly has its parts
Hidden gem
That make your day
And ugly is easy
So eager to please me
So quick to the lay
So if you're too hot
I'll just walk away

Shocked You Took the
Shock You Took

Loving you
For the noise that you make
The way you cry
When you try to make a brake
Braving the fence
A thousand watts
Makes your whole body tense
With a quiver
A lot of juice
That fence delivers
You twitch and rock
Till I've seen enough
And turn it off
Watching you drop
Always amazed
When up you hop
And I let you run
Far enough
That I can still
Hear you holler
When I turn
On the shock collar

Pants on Two Legs at a Time

Loving you
You're the man
And that alone
Makes me uncomfortable

Skipping a Beat

Loving you
On a day
That is not
Your turn
God I'm tired
Really
Feeling the burn
My other
Lover
Will be pissed
If I can't perform
You ain't seen anger
Till you've been in that storm
The on-the-side sex
Has gotta stop
It can't persist
I'm losing my hair
And killing my wrists
Shooting pure air
And breaking my arms
It ain't good for me
It's doing me harm
I no longer know
Right
From wrong
But from now on
I think it's best
If I only use
My left

Head

I gave my love
A chance to run
But dogs can hold a grudge
You're just lucky
They were small
And didn't eat you
Much at all
But left enough
For me to keep
My sweet little piece
Of torn up meat
I like to say
Our love is rare
But you never find that funny
I like to sit you on my lap
And pretend that you're my
dummy
Which you like even less
But I'll confess
It really gets me hot
Seems I love what you still have
And don't miss
What you ain't got
I'm sorry that you met with
harm
Someday
You won't miss that arm
Or that chunk from your ass
On the bright side of things
You're no longer passing gas
This change in you
Does not spell doom
Just think of all the elbowroom
You have without your elbows
The legroom you've gained

Without that leg
I swear
Someday
I'm gonna make you
The world's most happy
Head

Who's the Dummy Now

Loving you
Right in two
But don't believe
A word I say
You were already unfettered
Though I tried
Long and hard
To get you back together
But you wouldn't stay
So we had a three-way
I called your top Heather
Your bottom is May
Which makes me that cool party
guy
Look out girls
I'm really fly
Not that I've been
With a girl
That's alive
But I could
Now that I'm cool
And when I have the money
But for now I'm lonely
Needing more company
Which I'll get
When the store
Throws away
Another dummy

Someday Daddy

When I think of love
I think
Of the bomb
When I think of commitment
I remember
How long
It's been
Since I've visited mom
Which is why
I chose
To be by my side
A woman
In such a state
Of ruin
Who'll be sent away
And most likely soon
Cause dad always looked so
happy
After they took mom away
I want
To be like that
Someday

Wrong Makes Thong

Loving you
Cause my mamma insists
I don't know why
She hates her sis
And I hated it
From the first time
Your mustache chaffed me
I do it only
Cause momma's scary
Afraid she'd bend
And not unfold me
I gotta find a way out
And my dad is just no help
He stays curled in a ball
Afraid to even yelp
So I've got to do it
All by myself
And I've got a plan
A little snip here
A little tuck there
I'll put on a dress
Stop being a man
It's either that
Or face my mom
I'd rather sit upon a bomb
Either way
My junk is gone
But this way
I can wear a thong

Clam Up

Loving you
Like a clam
Here I am
In your shell
God it's hot
Hot as hell
Let me out
Let me out
Set me free
Trapped inside
A stinky clam
In not a place
For me
It's so dark
And you're all tongue
There isn't room
For my stuff
Let me out
I've had enough

Love is Hard

Loving you
Cause I've drunk way too much
The only thing cuming
Is what I'm throwing up
And though it is hot
I am not
I can't make it stand
Or see the strip
Where it needs to land
I'm not even sure
I'm not on the floor
Alone
Humping a stool
In the corner of the bar
Which would be embarrassing
If I could still get hard

September

Vending Machine of Love

One nut
Two nuts
Three nuts
More
I was supposed
To be quintuplets
But I loved
The other four
So much that
I digested their mass
Or rather I absorbed
Making one giant me
And the others are no more
Except for what you see
It wasn't feticide
It's working together
I keep them deep inside
Let's say we are tethered
Through four beating hearts
Seven out-stretched hands
Two brains
In three heads
Forty toes
On seven legs
Six extra nipples
Forty scattered dimples
And 26 moles
Now if you don't mind
Let's talk about holes
I've an inny
An outy

An outy
An inny
Selection is something
I got all about me
If you can't find it here
You ain't looking hard
I'm in no way deformed
Just erotically marred

Relieved

Loving you
Because
The bathroom is closed
And I gots to go
Half hoping
You don't find out
Half hoping
You already know
I chose you
Because you had enough room
I was in a rush
But I'll be done soon
When I've filled you up
I'll let you drop
Like a log
Wearing too much blush
Leaving you
With a courtesy flush

That's Not the Kind of Job
I'm Looking For
(Labor Day)

If you wanted
Me to work
You shouldn't
Have let me
On the bottom

Don't Push Till I Pull

Loving you
Through
The contractions
Cause
I'm dying
For some kind of action
When you scream
I know
It's not
That I'm so big
Don't think
I do not understand
But when you're yelling
Get it out
I feel
Like I'm
The man

Prenuptually Yours

Loving you
You have no choice
My only weapon
Is my voice
You're such a louse
It was easy to catch you
Cheating on your spouse
That poor faithful man
Always calling you honey
His dick in his hand
And oozing with money
Oh, don't look so shocked
Really it's funny
If you only could see
If you were only me
Holding your blouse
Don't try to object
That's not what I want
From inside your mouth
Don't bother with threats
Don't try to beg
I wrote it all down
So just spread your legs
Like you'll be doing
Every other day
For the rest of his life
If you cheat on the rich
You must pay the price

No Play No Pay No Way

I came upon
A came upon
That ventured to know me
I trod upon her underfoot
Cause she could see right
through me
She had no right
To look at me that way
I never promised that I'd stay
I wanted things to be easy
As I started getting hard
But I knew that it could never be
I'd have to buy the farm
I tried to explain
With a striking glance
That I only wished to rent the
plow
For a shady afternoon
I only wished to know
The way the field would rise
beneath me
As I burrowed
Raising furrows
Land turned into sea
Under me
Then when I knew as much of
that crop
As little interest would tell
I'd return the yoke and whip
Tie my shoes
And flap my lip
Goodbye I'd say
I'd like my deposit back
And right away
Please return my soul

And the freedom that I lent
To pay for the plow
Or rather
For the rent
But I knew that it could never be
I'd have to buy the farm
So I resigned myself
To another night
Of plowing
With my arm

One More Gasp for the Road

I was dreaming
Yesterday
Of how to take
Your breath away
I opted
For arsenic
What a kick
From a little lick
Tiny bit
Did the trick
I'll confess
I am impressed
First time
I've ever
Left you
Speechless

Socket To Her

I would love
To love
A socket
With my special rocket
And feel it straight
Up to
My brain
And though it may kill me
I am sure
That it
Will thrill me
As I get off on the pain
I used
To use a pen
Retracting now and then
What was a special friend
Goes away
When I come again
Leaving me with empty pockets
And a longing
For a socket
That has a special name
I call her Luricai
And I swear that I will miss her
Cause I really like the pain
To make a short
Story long
I don't think that it is wrong
I love her with all my heart
We can't stand
To be apart
I think that she is finger lickin'
When I'm plugged
And she starts kickin'
And I come until I came

It drains all my power
And I smell like burning flowers
I will never be the same

Loving Yew

Loving you
Like I do
When we visited
The zoo
Alone with the goats
Or the apes
Or a yew
And my dick
At the fence
Just poking through
With a little bread
On the end
Attracting a beastly slew
Among which
Always
I find you
For the zoos where we met
And the zoos where you stay
And here comes security
To chase me away
But I'll be back
Later today
Loving yew
Through the fence
At the zoo

Debtor's Prison of Love

I've owned you
For a week
And still you don't speak
Any English
You're so sweet
I'd love to take a bite
But that's strictly forbidden
Or so it's been written
Into the contract
So is love
At first sight
But the moment
You were unwrapped
I lost that fight
I know it's too soon
I feel like a sap
But I won't take you back
Not to that damn saloon
If I'd left you there
You'd probably be dead
At least that's what I whisper
When you're giving me head
I know
You do not understand
But I swear it makes you grin
Either that
Or you're biting in
Which I don't mind
As long as you're mine
As you work off your debt
A dime at a time
Though I hope
And I think
Am willing to bet
That the day will come

You'll love me yet
At least
By the time
You've worked off
Your debt

Let Me Expleen

Loving you
Though your mind
Is infirm
I don't care
What's not there
I don't mind
You don't learn
I'm not into your brain
What I love most of all
Can only be found
If I turn you around
And I know
You're too dumb
To know what I mean
When I say you're my love
And I love only spleen
Yours is the biggest
Voluptuous
Delicious
So terrific
That it leads
When we dance
Like Ginger and Fred
Though now that dream's dead
It won't continue
It can't
Since I found out
Your spleen
Is just an implant

Nothing Scratched Nothing Gained

Loving you
So damn quick
That if you had
An itch
I could have you
Once
Twice
Three times
More
And be well
Out the door
Before you
Could so much as
Twitch

There are Flowers Either Way

Today is the day
Let's bow our heads
And pray
I think it's rare
Suck a day
The people in black
The sky is gray
And your dress
Still dripping red
Still believing
We'll soon be wed
While everyone knows
I'm already dead

What Kind of End is

Insert name here
And me
Sitting in a deforested zone
Exchanging a mutual form of
herpes
First comes tongue
Then comes diarrhea
Then the cancer sets in
The end
Unless they cut
Your ass off in time
In which case
No end

Once Upon a Time When Parts Were Tight

There was a time
When
You were fine
Now
You're mine
There was a time
That
You were hot
Now you're not
Once you were a catch
Now you're caught
If we could only go back
Before you were mine
I'd cut the line

Nocturnal

Loving you
Like a bat
That lives deep
In a cave
Coming out
Late at night
For bug
Fruit or vein
Loving you
With a lust
That begins after dusk
And a couple of beers
I show up at our door
And I pound
And I pound
While you hide
And pretend
That you're not around
And the cops will be called
By you
Or a neighbor
And I yell
And I scream
I'll be seeing you later
And they take me away
Back to the cave
Where I'll sleep through the
morning
And most of the day
Just like any good bat
I won't attack
And I won't bite
Until it is
Once again night

Out of Uniform

I love
A man
In uniform
But your skates
Tear up
My bed
But I don't care
As I said
I love
A man
In uniform
But your junks
So well protected
Like a buried rock
I'm hoping for a bolder
But all I find is a jock
Till I roll you over
And I find the missing lump
Painfully erected
Bless my luck
You fill that cup
As I said
I love a man
In uniform
But when you shed your gear
It's as I feared
My lust goes dead
You're just a man
Out of my bed!

Exotic

You once
Loved a man
From Peru
Or maybe
The bottom
Of a shoe
One of the two
Which
I think
Is how I got
The tapeworm
Ain't exactly sure how it
happened
Don't want to learn
I should have known better
The way your privates
Squirmed

Pop and Fresh

Loving you
With a ding
And a pop
That's what I need
To get my rocks off
A pop
And a ding
Won't do
Not when it comes
To loving you

Yours and Miner

You are the sand
In my vagina
That I'll make
Into a pearl
You are the coal
In my crack
And I'm squeezing
Out the black
You are the encephalitis
Churning in my gut
Some say I'm sick
Others say I am a nut
But I'll turn your disease
Into whatever I please
And soon you will be
Pleasing me

Do Those Legs Go All the Way to the Bottom

Loving you
When I'm low
So I know
There's always lower
I can go
And when you
Come for seconds
Though I want us to be through
I always do
Cause when we're done
I can pinpoint
Down to the letter
The moment that life
Began to get better

Rosey in Red

I love all the girls
All the time
Using only my mind
And sometimes my hand
Except in the places
I'm currently banned
Like the schools
And the bars
The parks, pools and streets
And most any place
Just a little bit dark
I'm not even allowed
In most places to park
Without a door to door
Police accompanied
Notification of every single
resident within a square mile
I don't get many smiles
Or as much tail as I might
If I was only allowed
Out at night
Or to join social websites
Or make unsolicited calls
Use the sidewalk
Or visit the malls
But I don't mind
I still have sex
All of the time
And it's never the same
I've given my hand
So many names
And I like them all
Quite a bit
Thanks to my hands
Personality split

Hot Air

You're full of me
I blew you up
I set you free
I felt you up
I didn't meant to be so fresh
I thought we had an
understanding
Still
I should have asked before
Now the inflate-a-cops
Are at my door
Pounding
Softly

For Good Reason

Loving you
Cause everyone else does
I hate to make up
My own mind
When you seem ready
All the time
I'm sure if I thought
About it
I'd do it anyway
Anything
To keep you
From thinking
That I'm gay

Everything and the Kitchen Sink

Loving you
With an eight-track
I found in the back
A road-flair
A baby seat
A broken chair
A baseball bat
Cause baby
You got room for that
As well as the kitchen sink
Never
Have I ever felt
I have such a little dink
Turning all of those tricks
Changed you more than you
thought
And I think
It's time to retire
You've little left
To be desired
And I'm not just saying that
As the husband
You've left limp
But as the man
That's going broke
Trying to be your pimp

Early Bird

Loving you
Starts my day
And I just
Like to say
It's too early
Go away

Dough Know

Loving you
Gently wrapped
In the embrace
Of a deep
Rich
Dough
You should know
Though
That I know
About Jon
And it won't be long
Before no one
Will find you
Ever
Anywhere
Around
Now I lay
You down to rest
I loosen my belt
It's time to digest

Dinners Hot and So Are You

Loving you
At the point
Of a knife
Baby
We're doing it
On the table tonight
Next time
Maybe
Let's clean it off first
Some of this shit
Really does hurt
Like the steaming hot gravy
And the ice-cold desert
And I think a string bean
Has reached
My spleen
I'm covered in croutons
And red-wine vinaigrette
You've got so many places
That feel warm and wet
And the turkey is wearing your
shoe
I'm not even sure
For exactly how very long
I mistook it
For being you

Golden Touch

Loving you
With a spoon
Stirring fast
Heavy falls first
And light particles last
What stays
On the bottom
Is gold
I'd cut you in
Don't want to seem cold
But what's mined
Is mine
At least in my mind
Though greed may be a sin
I hope you don't mind
I dug right in
And the profits
Are making me
Richer than sin
Still I feel I own you something
I hate to let you down
But my claims been jumped
And I'm leaving town
It ain't like being dumped
Cause Tony
Will be here
On Tuesday
Only he don't care
For the scenery
He's bringing in
The heavy machinery

Head

Loving you
Unintentionally
I only asked to come on up
So I could take a pee
I never thought
When I got up
You'd want me to take me higher
But it really wasn't a good time
To light up my desire
You're beautiful
I couldn't say no
My bladder was full
I had to go
You climbing on me
I told you so
Please oh please
I begged of you
Let me use the toilet
But you said
This was raw hot sex
And leaving now
Would spoil it
So I went
Deep inside
Your over heated vent
That weren't so hot
When I got through
So fine
Wish I were dead
It never would have happened
Had you let me
Use the head

October

Deep Red Love Flows

Loving you
Through a hole
That I made
In my head
I'd be dead
If it weren't
For the love
In my head
That flows red
Through the hole
Where our love
Is contained
And I know
It is real
By the pain
That I feel
In my head
Where our love
Was revealed
Where I carved
A deep hole
Like a heart
In my soul
It goes all
The way through
Like all love should do
In my head
Where my love
Will always
Flow red

Cheapers Creapers

Loving you
For a fee
That seems really small
When you're as loaded as me
It's near nothing at all
I got more allowance
Every damn day
Then you cost a week
And that was when I was twelve
Now I'm thirteen
And rich as hell
So keep in line woman
For any mess I make
I can certainly clean
If you know what I mean
And if you don't
Just know I pay extra
For a noose and a rope
And don't image
We're some sort of lovers
Or I'll plant you out back
In the woods
With the others

Deli Counter

Chicken loved a turkey
Turkey loved a ham
Ham loved a man
The only part of this whole mess
I even understand
Cause that man
Is a pig
And probably a chicken
And a rat at that
He stole my woman
And I ain't taking that
Which is why I tied him to the
log
Dressed him real pretty
And left him for the hog
To the horror of the chicken
And the delight
Of the ham
And the horror of my woman
Though I'll never understand
How you could love a rat
That is so full of bacon
Oh what a ride
That ass has taken
A man can never understand
The fairer sex
Or who it is she may select
But no one will ever love you
like I have
And you may think it coarse
But that is why I tied you up
Lashed you to the fence
And then unleashed
The horse

It Seemed Like a Good Idea
at the Time

Loving you
Incoherently
Monkey chestnut
Rock strewn knee
Santa clause
Tuna fish
Chicken hawk
What a dish
Loving mustard pie
Cry
Thigh
My
My my
My my my my
Pass out
Probably
Die

Finders Keepers

I found you
So I'll keep you
You should never
Have gotten
So lost
I'll build a place
To keep you
No matter what the cost
Though
I'll probably
Just put you
With the others
And tell them all
That you're their mother

Dollar for Dollar

Loving you
Every day
Is how
I spend my pay
Every dollar
Every day
And you don't even holler
You don't even care
You don't even act
Like you know I'm even there
It's more than I can take
Is more than I can stand
Which is probably why
I release in my hand
Or sometimes my sock
I rarely have the time
To pull out the rock
And put it to your world
To make you feel like I'm the
man
And you're a little girl
But I don't last
Long enough
Even to annoy
Which is probably why
You always ask
For the money upfront

Diamond in the Flaw

I was hit
By a bus
And woke up
With you
The things you find
On the side of the highway
The things people throw away
A perfectly good man
An almost good man
I'm damaged
Still
I don't understand
One woman's treasure
Was a bus driver's trash
If she can't fix me
She'll sell me for cash
For another man's leisure
I better work fast
Finding a way to please her
Ownership
Is nine tenths of the law
It's my own damn fault
I'm worth less than my flaws

Dickotomy

Loving you
From the front
And behind
At the same time
Might seem
Hard to do
But my dicks
Sliced in two

36 – 14 – 92
(Columbus Day)

Loving you
Like Columbus
I killed your family
And put you to work
Sometimes
Love hurts
Sometimes
It makes us its slave
And sends us to
An early grave
Leaving one
Left behind
With nothing to hold
Except maybe
A ton of gold

Two Horns for Every Boy
(Leif Erikson Day)

Loving you
Like a Viking
Grabbing
And dragging
Any girl I am liking
Back
To my boat
Where I'll teach you
How it feels
Had you been born
A goat
Where brutal
And cruel
Are good
For a start
If you could act sicker
You may win my heart
Or at least
Be done quicker
And I might set you free
If you can get
My horned
Helmet
All the way
Inside me

Desire's Fire Needs a Cool Compress

I've a fire
That burns
Only for you
That relights
Every time
I need to make poo
A blaze
Ablaze
A deep hole of fire
If itch
Is the yard stick
Then I've got a mile
Of pure
Undeterred
Unadulterated
Desire

Doctor is as Doctor Does

Loving you
Cause the doctor
Said I'm okay
He said all the bumps
Will soon go away
It could be what I'm eating
Or maybe shampoo
Or maybe baby
It could be from you
But I'm gonna be fine
He's willing to bet
And if symptoms persist
He says see a doctor
And not just
A vet

Diet Men You

Loving you
Steamed
Never fried
After fighting with mom
That's how my dad died
So I like my girls healthy
It's hard to throw steam
I like my girls skinny
It takes the edge out of mean
When things get too hot
I run
From stoves
From oil
And I ain't coming back
Till things ain't at a boil
So baby
Though you're my heart's desire
If there's hot oil near
Don't light my fire

Tools for Fools

Gave my love a hammer
And she smashed my toes
Gave my love a hatchet
And she gashed my nose
Fool me once
Shame on you
Fool me twice
Then I'm the fool
If I don't hide
All my tools

Ditched

Loving you
Is not that wrong
If it isn't that long
Loving you
Ain't that sick
If I choose the right ditch
If you're never found
Then you're still around
Most likely
A whore in Tennessee
At least
Last time I saw you
Last time you saw me
That's where you said
You were gonna be
I'm expecting a phone call
Any day
Once she's found a place
To stay
Unless she's back on the coke
At least that's the best
Her family can hope
That's she's out turning tricks
And not just fucked
Then dropped in a ditch

No Need for Words

Loving you
Twice a day
For over an hour
For nearly
One day
In a row
You don't have to thank me
Baby
I already know

Roll Over Rover

Loving you
Like the dog
That I kept
In my yard
Not too long
Not too hard
So the cops won't be called
Since you're really too small
Like the dog in my yard
That I can't fuck too hard
Or I'd break him in two
Which is more
Then I want
I can barely stand you
I'd hate
If you
Were suddenly two
Twice as thin

Roll Over Rover Redux

Loving you
Like the dog
That lay dead
In the yard
Loved too long
Loved too hard
Leaving both of us
Scared
And when we land
Only one
Is still able to stand
It's me
I'm the man
Back to loving my hand
But at least
It's not two
Of you
Twice as thin

Four Score and Twenty to One

I ain't met a girl
Like you
Since 1892
The way you sat
Right on my lap
Your hips always
On the move
Rubbing places
I forgot I had
My hands working fast
For my age
And before I know
We are engaged
Even though
I know you cheat
Even though
I know you lie
It won't be long
Before I die
Quickly we'll marry
Soon I'll be buried
There's no time
Left for doubt
You'll end up rich
Wealthy as hell
Just as long
As you keep putting out

Returns Good for Store Credit Only

I told the cops
It wasn't my idea
It was that little man
That took all my money
And told me to chop you up
Sorry honey
I always planned
To grow you back
A bunch of you
In fact
The little man promised that
As long as I used
His magic serum
I could turn
You into a harem
Now you're just
A bunch of meat
It's a good thing
I kept
The receipt

Empty Inside

Loving you
Through a friend
That I hollowed out
For the occasion
He promised
To help me
Make your relations
But that is not
The only part I needed
And now I'll never
Get him back together
Instead
I'll chew him
Into the softest leather
And continue
Loving you
Forever

Rat Sack Carrot Smack

My love
Won't share
Her carrots
Never get involved
With a ferret
They're cheap
They horde
And they act
Like rats
Their only redemption
They're good
In the sack
Done

Loving you
With a fork
Just to see
If you're done
I don't care
About rare
I like mine
Well done
Not simply broiled
But seared by the sun
And before it is over
You'll wish you'd rolled over
And taken it
Into your bum
Which was my original plan
Before I had to switch
To this
Scorched by the sun
Fork if it's done idea
Which isn't bad either

Falling For You

Loving you
As we fall
I don't like you
Not at all
But as the ground
Grows near
You've become quit dear
To my heart
After we hit
I'm sure
They'll never get us apart
Or know what part
Belonged to who
Or who
Is missing parts
So I better get
Use to you
And what better way to start
Before my ribs surround your
heart
Than a quick game
Of hide the gator
Before we're nothing
But a crater

Funky Smelling Jeans

There are ways I love you
But none of them are clean
You're so warm and broken
Like my funky smelling jeans
I've worn away your color
You fit me like a glove
And although you've gotten
moldy
You're still the one I love
You're tearing at the seams
Getting kinda beat
You're frayed at the cuff
And ripped along the seat
You still fell like a woman
Except you're not so mean
Someday I'll have to patch you
That's just how much you mean
I'll never wear another
You cost way too much
You look just like my mother
And that will always be
Enough

One Dreamer, Put it on the Card

I never dreamed
We'd be together
Till I learned
How much you
Earned
Now I dream
Now I burn
And probably yearn
Or something
Whatever it is
You want to hear
Whatever it takes
To draw you near
Cause there's a lot of people
Depending
On this union
There's a whole heap of people
That keep
Praying hard
Like my family
My friends
And MasterCard

Eulogy

Loving you
Cause you died
And you won't need your eyes
Loving you cause you're dead
And you won't need your head
Loving you
Though you've passed away
But with a little gravy
I can love you anyway
Either way
Every way
All night and all day
At least till the gravy has dried
Or the authorities find out
That you have died

Done on Time

Loving you
Cause my new names'
Bend Over
Though some on the block
Been callin' me Rover
And some
Just 'Bout To Get The Bone
No matter how you slice it
I'm the prettiest girl
In all of lockdown
My life hasn't turned
Out like I thought
I'm not a stud
I am a fox
I'm not a business mogul
But I'm making a good livin'
Here in prison

Growing on Me

Loving you
Despite the rash
That goes down to your knees
Loving you
Though I have
No sign of disease
Loving you
Despite the limitations of
antibiotics
You're near
That's what I need
And the rash rarely bleeds
Yes
I'm really that lonely
But not that cleaver
Whatever you give me
I'll have forever
Sometimes loves itches
And sometimes love burns
And sometimes you get
More than you earned
But with you I'll earn
All that I get
And when I get sick
I'll know
You'll always be with me
Whatever I grow

Her Hand

I'm calling
To ask
For your daughter's hand
I've already eaten
The rest
You raised
One delicious
Young lady
And I'm hoping
Just maybe
You've bred some more
Don't think that I'm a pervert
I'm a connoisseur
I'd gladly trade
A blowjob
For a baguette
Don't think it's sick
Depraved
Or sad
Nothing tastes better
Than a meal
That you've
Already had

Your Persona is Showing (Halloween)

Please
Keep the costume
On
There's nothing I like better
Than a real good con
And I think
It would be fun
I've never had
A pregnant nun
At least not one
With a jack-o-lantern face
Eyes that glow
A belly that screams
A tail with a point
And disentailed spleen
Something about it
Is so sultry
If I don't know
Who you are
Then it isn't adultery
On this bewitched night
On the most ghostly day
I'm gonna take you the other
way
You're lucky
I decided
To dress
Like I'm gay

November

Moving too Fast to Not Fall

Loving you
Though it took
A long time
You ran so damn fast
And you were so hard to find
That if I hadn't heard
That whimpering whine
I may not have loved you at all
And it's not my fault
You had such a long fall
Hit so many rocks
Or landed on a mower
It never would've happened
If you'd only run slower
And you'd had more
Strength to fight
Which I have to admit
Is the part that I like
But I brought you home anyway
For many a night
And many a day
Till I release you next time
When I willing to bet
You won't run so fast
Or be so hard to find

Hit Man Comes Home

Warning
Loving me
May cause
Bodily harm
Don't be alarmed
I'm not cruel
Just a fool
Who loves like a mercenary
Don't take it personally
You're just on my list
The torture begins
Before the first kiss
Which was never supposed
To be with my fist
My loving embrace
Always does damage
Damage right to the face
And if I ever make it inside
I'll be amazed
If you survive
Fortunately
That's not part of my criteria

Drive Through

Loving you
On the side
Like my fries
Supper sized
I don't want
Just a shake
What I want
Is shake and bake
And extra layer
An extra coat
Some extra gravy
To float my boat
Some extra fodder
For the goat
So when we're done
Done in the sack
I don't have to wander
Far for a snack
There's enough of you
To go around
With the right sauce
You're the best girl
In town

Fill Till Empty

They said
I'd always be alone
Because I have no brain
I don't know what they mean
I'll always have a bone
They're really just the same
And when I took you home
You seemed to agree
A bone
Was good enough for you
And that's good enough for me
It's nice to have
Someone who
Isn't thinking too
We're so dumb
It's a calamity
Let's get married
And raise a family

Marrying Man

I'd like to ask
For your daughter's hand
In marriage
No
I don't care
Which one
And just to show
I'm sporting
I'll even take
A son

Love is Just Your Condition

I love you
You don't love me
It don't make sense
Your love's not free
But master
To your slave
Is not what I'm after
You're supposed to relate
Fall in love
With your captor
I even keep you
In a cage
Instead of love
I get rage
How long
Does this hate
Go on
Where's the compassion
Where's the bond
I'm tired
Of all the abuse
I chose the wrong disorder
All of this
Is of no use
Maybe if I were
A different sick
You could nurse me
In my home
At my bedside all alone
And from there
Our love would grow
Sparkling
Glimmering
Covered in chrome
As I keep you near
Whispering softly in your ear
Welcome to your home
Thank you
Oh thank you
Florence Nightingale
Syndrome

Hosing Posing Rose's Nose

Love is a hose
So you better
Not run
It over
With a lawnmower
Love is a nose
So you better
Not blow it
Love is a pose
But if you strike it
They'll arrest you
Then love becomes
A rose
That grows
In the prison block
That blooms
Wherever you stand
On demand

Behind You All the Way

Zip
Zam
Zoo
I loved you in the loo
And I don't mean
The place you pee
I mean
The place
You poo
But it's not for the sex
That's not the part I dig
It's the way
You always yell
Oh god
It's just too big
And I thank you for that
And I'm sorry for that
But it's the whole reason
I keep coming back

Drumstick

Loving you
Like a duck
Cause I love to flock
Loving you
Like a chicken
Cause I'm such a cock
Loving you
With giblets and gravy
We'll call it Thanksgiving
And eat all our babies
Just like we did
When we were kids

Seaman's Semen Sees Only Seamen
(Veteran's Day)

Loving you
While your man is
Away
He joined the navy
He's probably
Gay
Either way
He's on a two-year cruise
So I'll keep warm
What he can't use
And when he's back
He'll know more
About killing
And less
How to act
So I'll run away
But I'll return
When I feel the burn
And we'll pretend
That we're just friends
Until
He ships out again

Family Prayer Time

I saw you
At the county fair
Through blinding light
And pounding thunder
I have to know
Oh my sweat one
What rock
Did you crawl out
From under
That you could be so much like
me
I think we should be lovers
You wear dirt so naturally
Like a hook
That's just been baited
I can only hope
And pray to god
I find out we're related

Good Past The Last Gasp

Loving you
At a time
When love
Just won't do
Sinking rapidly
Into
The deep icy blue
But if I take a breath
Just before we go under
I think
I can see
This thing through
By thunder

Making You Melt One Way or Another

Loving you
In the rain
Betting
That you'll melt
Loving you
With a noose
I made
From my belt
The way you moaned
I quickly knew
You liked the way
It felt
Loving you
With a hammer
Barely left
A welt
Loving you
With a mallet
Is how
The final
Blow
Was dealt
A little acid
Beats the rain
And now
You're flowing
Down the drain

Moo to You

Loving you
Like a heifer
Anywhere
And whenever
And I love the way you moo
Truth be told
I moo you too
I lay you down in the hay
Really it's the only way
Cause then you can't get up
But I sure can
And I don't let up
Till you've had enough
Which can take a real long time
Your sex organs
Are much bigger than mine
I work in both hands
And most of a foot
And don't stop
Till I've lost my shoe
It's the easiest way
To tell when we're through
And just like a man
I leave you there
You calling my name
I pretend I don't hear
I'm way too small
To hoist a steer

Last Wishes, One After the Other

Loving you
Because
I ran you over
And I figure
You'd want it
One more time
Before you die
And the cops agree
So do the paramedics
And a biker gang ridding by
As well as six truckers
A U-Haul stuffed with
immigrants searching for a better
life
A bus-load of college kids
returning from a stellar second
place finish at the Milwaukee
State Marching Band Finals
Three old drooling ladies
And a squirrel
And I'm betting
You live a long time
Since I didn't hit you hard
Hardly taped you
Really only scratched you
Or maybe a bruise
Still pinned under my tire
We all agree
Your closeness to death
Really lit your fire
So sit back
Enjoy the ride
And be grateful
You're still alive

A Short Apology

Loving you
With a bat
That I keep
By the door
Just because
I mistook you
For an unscrupulous whore
And the only cure
Is to bludgeon your sin
As you walked in
To prove I love you the most
That I love you more
That's why I swung
As you walked through the door
It's the love I keep
Buried deep down within
That allowed me
To smite you
Again and again
And again and again
And again and again and again
Till what was left
What remained
In a heap on the floor
Was no longer a whore
But sweet tender bits
Of the girl I adore
I don't think you are less
But very much more
And I'll never again
See you as that whore
That I bashed by the door
Especially since the district
attorney explained to me you
never cheated

And I was only having a
delusional episode
Brought on by a twelve day
meth binge
So I wanted to let you know
After careful consideration
I accept your apology
And love you baby
And all your associated bits

Happy Forever

Loving you
Most
When we're not
Together
Loving you
Best
When I'm all alone
I way on you
Like a feather
You gnaw on me
Like a bone
I have a closet
I lock myself in
I won't answer
When you ask
Where have you been
Don't get me wrong
We can be happy
Forever
Just keep away
And talk to me
Never

Cold Meat Served Hot

Loving you
During the war
While you
Lay in the morgue
Loving you
You looked tough
But barely warm
To the touch
I kept a fire burning
Under the butt
I won't let you get cold
I like my men hot
And juicy
Tender and delicious
Without any bugs
Or rigamortis
Still I fear
Our love will not keep
You'll be packed
In a box
In less than a week
Then all I'll have
To remember you by
Is a few pieces
Your family won't miss
Something to hold
Something to ride
Something to kiss
Altering the report
To read
That you were blow
To bliss

A Wiener Every Time

It's my first time
In a place like this
It had to happen
I can't resist
From the first time I saw
Her walking the street
I began to stuff
My pants with meat
Jiggling around
Keeping it raw
Blood dripping down
A pool on the ground
As I describe
To the attendant
How I saw you walking
Out on the street
He knew you right away
Arranged us to meet
And for a nominal fee
I took you home
And set you free
Free to jump all over me
And eat
And eat
And eat
Blessed be the day
That I found
The local pound

Gonna Wash That Girl

Loving you
Now that the bleeding
Has stopped
Loving you
Cause the yelling
Didn't bring
The cops
Now you know why
Instead of flowers
I brought
A mop

Hot Pepper Behind

I scratched out my eyes
And still
I see you
Don't know
How you stand
Seeing you too
I can't tell your ass
From your face
I always choose wrong
When I'm spraying the mace
Everything you do
Makes me mad
I can't wait
Till you meet
My mom
And my dad

Gobble Gobble Means I Love You (Thanksgiving)

I found you
With a turkey
Always gobbling
In your ear
But I made that bird
Disappear
You don't deserve
Anything so poultry
You're too delicious
So brown
And sultry
You're mud colored eyes
Look right through me
The sweetest chick
With a lousy bird
You smell like flowers
He looked like a turd
You are an angel
He was a dick
Now you're my girl
Have another
Drumstick

Sick About You

You got mine
And I got yours
I can tell by the open sores
Just like love
Our puss must grow
Just like love
From head to toe
We are nearly one
The way we stick
You're the only one
I can't get sick
Quarantine
Ain't no dream
But at least I got you baby
Together we got everything
Mashed with a stick of rabies
I hope that we can make this
love
Last damn near forever
Cause they ain't gonna let us out
Anytime
No time
Never

Cosmically Like Forever

Loving you
Across the eons
At least
That's how it feels
Like we've traveled
A million miles
In stiletto heels
Getting fat
Widening thighs
From a lifetime of meals
We're not really alive
Slowly we work
At a poor plot to die
To get the deal done
Sure in our next life
We'll start having fun

Crickety Crack

Loving you
So high on crack
My penis
Just won't react
So please
Can I have
My money back
I'd really
Like to
Buy more crack

Nothing Makes Me Crazy

Baby you know
I'm crazy for you
I'd have to be
You don't exist
Yet you set me free
The night that we first kissed
Me not holding you in my arms
Embracing empty air
Pulling it near
And I whisper sweet nothing
In your nothing there
Then moving in with my mouth
Breathing you in
And steaming you out
And just because you are not
there
Doesn't mean
I didn't feel
The treads of air
That you dared
To call underwear
Always the temptress
My hands fumbling at your
dress
And you always pushing away
I didn't know
Nothing
Was so hard to get
At any rate
I'm willing to wait
Cause baby
For you
I am crazy

Crusty Satisfaction

Loving you
Really poorly
I mean really damn bad
Less than blah
Worse than bleck
Really quite sad
And I think
I'll just quit
Neither one of us
Seems to enjoys it a bit
I'll say that I'm sleepy
I'll claim that I'm through
And if you love me
You'll say that you're done too
And we'll go right to sleep
Swearing
There's no more we can do
Could do
Would do
Till in our dreams
Where we're young
Full of vigor
I'll be with someone perky
You'll be with someone bigger
And we'll both wake up
Satisfied
Wiping sex
Out of our eyes

Daddy's Girl

Loving you
Like my last day
My last day to live
Which it could be
Though I feel
I've so much more to give
I was supposed to have you back
Back home by ten
And not one minute more
That from your daddy
Who's already
Cut me before
But what's a boy to do
When his daughter's a whore
But learn the fastest
Route to the door
And then straight out of town
Before he makes me
No longer around

Icy Came the Thaw

Loving you
In the freezer
Snowy cones
Ice-cold beaver
My favorite parts
Snap right off
So I can keep them
When I go
A memento
From my ice cold ho
That I loved so raw
It nearly lasted
Till the thaw

Cow and Cognito

Loving you
When the cows
Come home
I can't get it up
If we are alone
There's something
About bovine
That makes a snake
A straight line
Which really isn't that weird
But it's also why
I cry
If you don't wear the beard

Cast Away

If I were to be stuck
On a deserted island
With only one person
I'd like it to be you
In the hardest of times
You'd always pull through
You'd feed me for months
And provide perfect shelter
With you near
I'd never feel alone
Then I'll make you into raft
And float your ass home

December

Bones About Me

There was a time
I thought you divine
Should never had said
You'd never be mine
I know you didn't mean
To piss me off
At least
That's what
I tell the cops
Who can't charge me
Till they find
A body
Maybe
A body that isn't there
Since I took the time
To show I care
Making sure we'd be together
I always want you near
So I kept you right here
Still I fear
I lose
A little of you
Every time I move
Soon I'll be all alone
If I ever
Pass your bones

Down the Voluptuous Drain

I know the way home
I just choose not to go
I know how to say yes
I just choose to say no
And still you follow me
Everywhere I go
Like a dog that's been kicked
By the shoe that it loves
Or a pigeon that longs
For the embrace of a dove
As it's hit by a car
Or shot from above
Or a dog that's been fixed
And dry-humps the cat
It's true what they say
Don't make love
To a rat

All That's Left Can Blow

Loving you
Like I'm a furry log
Mostly decayed
From years in a bog
Full of bugs and worms
Ready to decompose
In your arms
My fine remains
Will slip between your toes
My dusty bits
Will get inside your nose
My termites and ticks
Will move into your holes
I feel I am ready
Ready to explode
But all that's left
Is the tip of my nose
But oh
How it blows

Bovine Spells Fine

Loving you
Like a cow
In my living room
I need something that shocks
And something that grooms
The first is for me
The second for you
Cause you ain't that good
looking
And take up too much room

Pop Knows Hot

Loving you
With some corn
You're so damn hot
I just know it's gonna pop
You're the hottest girl
I've ever used
If not for the corn
I'd be chewing on you
Don't be bitter
I couldn't love
You better
If you came with butter
We were meant
For one and other
It's not a fad
Not a phase
I'll love you
As long
As you
Pop
My maze

Rubba Dubba Done

Loving you
Like a tuna
Slick and fast
Then throw you back
And take a bath

All That and a Bag

You're the bag of chips
Without all that
You're the shaved rabbit
That looks like a rat
You're the fair-haired maiden
That's lunch-buffet fat
I don't know what more to say
I've done everything I can
And you won't go away
Even after I spent six months
Living like I'm gay
Boy
What a pain in the ass
But it seemed like the only way
Still
You stay
Attached like glue
Taking beatings
Ignoring pleadings
Swearing if I thought it best
I could cut you with a knife
I guess I best just settle down
And take you
As my wife
And do anything you say
For the rest of my life

All You Left is Gone

When last I saw you
It was Sunday
Never had so much fun
I never thought
That come Monday
You'd tell me that we're done
I've been a day
Since
You've gone away
Oh how will I get through?
I've already scrapped and
snorted
All of your residue
Today is only Monday
What's a man to do
I've licked every single thing
That even smells like you
Now I'm left with nothing
Oh how will I get through
Today is only Monday
And I've taken
All of you

Bruised at Best

To the victor
Goes the spoils
I only wish
That you were fresher
There's such a thing as overripe
If I'd have know
Your state of rot
I would have thrown the fight

Captive Heart	Catch and Release
Loving you	Loving you
Like I have a choice	I'm a cop
Loving you	And you've been caught
Like there's a voice	Running lights
Echoes of love	Packing pot
Stuck in my head	An outstanding warrant
Instead of your father	While looking real hot
Swearing I'm dead	So late at night
If I ever hurt you	On a quiet back road
A similar threat	You didn't fight
Led to I do	You found a way
Just because	To pay
You had a kid	What was outstanding
And I'm among	Now your warrants
The possible dads	Have been repealed
Dumbest thing I ever did	I'm throwing that in
Next to fleeing slower	It wasn't part of the deal
Than your daddy nabbed	Please
This will be the ruin of me	Speed this way again
And is bound to ruin her	Any time you're wanted
A whale of a problem	And you'll lose a strike
That could have been avoided	For every at bat
If the man that harpoon her	Unless
Had only pulled out sooner	Of course
	You've gotten fat

Easy Going Guy

I have the heart
Of a child
Under my pillow
I have the soul
Of a toddler
I bought from the devil
That's probably why I'm so
mellow
I hardly
Ever
Nearly
Never
Kill a fellow
And it's been
A real long time
Since
I hit a bitch
I do less wrong
I can control the itch
I only need one more soul
If I can collect it
And everything
Should be
Copasetic

Soft as Fast can Be

Loving you
Crack crack crack
With the hitting side
Of my wiffle-ball bat
Loving you
Boom boom boom
With the softest tip
On my harpoon
Loving you
Quick quick quick
Cause my shows
Coming on
And I'm getting off
So if you want love
That's really great
You'll have to wait
Till a commercial break

Throw Another Log on my Baby

Lake of Fire's
Where we met
And it ain't got
Colder yet
And we're still
No closer to god
I say what the hell
Throw on another log
I'm not just fallin'
I already fell
And nothing could be better
Let's burn in hell
Together

Beauty Starts Within

Loving you
In a way
That you'll poop
Before we lay
Anywhere near each other
Or I'm not going to pay
Hey
Wait
Don't go away
I've a big chocolate heart
I've made just for you
I like my girls clean
All the way through
Don't worry you'll live
And your sin will be flushed
Flushed clean away
Then you'll get
Everything
That I got to give
Bu not till after
The laxative

Landing Clearance Granted

I remember
The day we met
Until I started drinking
From then on
It's a little fuzzy
But I recall clearly
Under risk of perjury
And can convince any jury
That you got undressed
On your own
That you said yes
And even moaned
And you're the one
That got me stoned
Which is why
We decide to fly
Your dad's plane
To the mall
And we would have made it
If we'd cleared that first wall

With And Without Starch

Loving you
In a dryer
Set
On permanent press
Lights my desire
And cleans up the mess
When lust
Meets with heat
That's when I start to holler
Does anyone here
Have change for a dollar

What Goes Out, Must Come In

May god save your soul
Cause it's sinking fast
When out of your hole
There came a great blast
A flash a light
A bit or rock
A plastic thing
Shaped like a cock
Three gold rings
And a flea collar
A pad with wings
Wrapped in twelve dollars
A diaphragm
A tube of glue
Something borrowed
And something blue
An old tire
A license plate
A bon fire
A long-lost date
A sunken ship
A bit of tin
And then the hole
It sucked back in
It sucked the light
It sucked the stars
It sucked the rock
It sucked the cock
It sucked the rings, the collars,
the wings, the dollars
It sucked the diaphragm, the can
of glue
Something borrowed, something
blue

The tire, the plate, the fire, the
date, the ship, the tin
Sucked it all right on in
Back on in
It all flew
The only thing
I've ever seen
That suck more
Is
You

Buy the Hour

Love is cheap
If you want to
Expensive
If you need
As long as the money
Is going toward education
And there's no soil
For my seed
I've only twenty dollars
To get what I need
But need $2,000
For what I desire
I hate to rent a lover
When I really want to buy her

It's What's For Dinner	Clinical Trial
Loving you	Loving you
With a fish	Is as queer
That was ticked	As a three dollar bill
Till death	It could be your beard
Then cooked	Or that you're thin pale and ill
With its head	When you ran away
Intact	I called from behind you
And it's ass	I don't know your name
Still in place	Oh how you will I find
In a light garlic sauce	Now that you've ditched
That was splashed in your face	All I have to trace you
The fish dropped	Is a well pronounced itch
In your pants	A fragment of sleeve
With a splash of lime	And a warm feeling inside
With a sprig of parsley	That is really disease
Then I give it some time	My god I love you
To see if it revives	And it's not just a line
Which ain't a good sign	Or some kind of gimmick
What's good for the fish	It's true love this time
Ain't good for the hog	Its size has no limit
A pool fit to swim	I'll search for you nonstop
Will just rot a log	At every free clinic
I'm not pointing fingers	
I didn't say the word whore	
Still	
I best be out the door	
For	
It's bad for my erection	
To be where anywhere near	
A fish resurrection	

Bound to Love Me

I'm not really
As bad
As the hidden cell
In my basement
Makes me look
The whole time you were captive
I didn't make you cook
Or clean
Or even make the bed
You always seemed tied up
And who provided for you all
those years
Keeping you in rags and crumbs
Nursing every fear
And it wasn't easy
I had other mouths to feed
It is a large basement
So don't think I don't love you
Or didn't care
That's the whole reason
I kept you there
And on that fact
I'll never budge
So if you have the time
Could you please
Tell the judge

The Ties That Fray

Loving you
You're my friend
I'm here till the very end
Just to make you suffer
That's what it means
To love one and other
You're the only one
I want to abuse
Not to throw away
Just over use
Like the rag thrown
At every damn mess
Till you pull out your hair
As I build a nest
No matter how
Banged up
Ruffed up
Battered
And bruised
I'll always see you
As just really used
I'll keep you forever
I'll never let us part
I'll always be near
Taking bites
From your heart

Chester's Nuts Roasting
(Christmas Eve)

Loving you
Before Christmas
All over the yard
The cold in the air
Made me excessively hard
Then I made a mistake
Calling you the wrong name
You locked the front door
And it started to rain
I banged on that door
With all of my might
It's Christmas Eve for god sakes
Let's not have a fight
It's freezing out here
I'll die's what I said
As all my belongings
Rained down on my head
You won't get away
You can't do this to me
When next to the house
I saw a large tree
You shouldn't make mountains
Of such a small goof
So I climbed up the tree
And dropped onto the roof
I thought how I'd hurt you
I thought how you'd scream
Then I slid down the chimney
As if in a dream
Yelling Santa's coming
So baby don't worry
But was met by a fire
And tried to climb up in a hurry
But up was not the direction for
me
And I slid back down
And burned up like a tree
Ending forever
My Christmas story

Can't Shake the Surprise
(Christmas)

Loving you
With some scissors
Some paper
Some tape
And a big red bow
This year
For the first time
Christmas
Isn't gonna blow
This year I started early
I found just the right thing
I wrapped it
And I hid it
Sometime late last spring
Nothing is too good for you
I bound
And gagged
And cut you
In two
It's been eight months
And you haven't been missed
I've already got
My Christmas wish

Bone Bone and Bone

I can't wait
Till we're alone
All that's left
Of you is bones
I've explained it
To your family
If they want all of you
They'll have to kill me
I for one
Am willing to share
I just need a piece
From here
There
And there
Of your bones
I only need three
Your father's the one
With too much greed
But selfishness
Don't pay the rent
And I got insurance
To collect
I gotta believe
There will be
Enough money
For three bones
And we'll finally get
Some time alone

Boiled Spoiled and Exiting the Ride

I'm a snail
Steamed in its shell
I'm a lobster
About to boil
Before I explode
I need a girl
That's really, really spoiled
One that's rotten to the core
To keep me in my place
Giving me what for
Through a candy face
She needs a hurricane inside
So if I look too at ease
She'll throw me
From the ride
So long
Good bye
With a swift kick in the bum
I need a girl
To get away from
So I can find a home
I've always needed someone
Now I need to be alone
And I think that you
Can really help
If you keep on acting
Like yourself

Hit Hard Enough to Make Little Ole You

To me you are the moon
Imagine
The boom
When I'm blindsided
Gashed and pocked
By a sky-born rock
And there you are
An unblinking eye
In a constant
Orbital taunt
As if you were a jaded lover
From a night
That I forgot
Forgot to use a rubber
And now you want child
support
Next time I'm launching
With the moon in my scope
To avoid further hurt
Before I cohort
I better abort

Replacement Part

Witches Broom
Make room
I'm now the thing
She rides
And more
I also clean the floor
I've muddied up
The hallway
Just to get some more
She's sometimes
My hero
She makes me eat soap
She's not quite a lady
She's Nero
On coke
I love her a lot
She calls me Marry
She's the best thing I got
She's the man
And I'm the fairy
And I didn't even know
Until she made me
Thank her
For telling me so
Whatever she asks
I just fall right in
Tomorrow may suck
I'm replacing the caldron
Wish me luck

Blind Man's Buff

Love is blind
At least
That's what I advertised for
The blind don't mind
And if they ask for more
You say
You just had it
Or it's sitting right there
Why don't you grab it
And when things turn
Kinda shitty
Just drop 'em off
In a distant city

All Year Wrong
(New Year's Eve)

Loving you
The whole year
Wrong
Bet you never knew
A year could last
So long
Soon I'll be gone
I'll let you escape
But you'll always remember
You're worst ever
Blind date
We shared more
Than abuse
There was sodomy
Which I did all for you
And not just for me
I had to make sure
You took all you could bare
Till living
Or dying
You really didn't care
All for tomorrow
When
For the first time ever
You'll have a happy New Year
And when you do
Think of me
And how I loved you
Horribly

www.ingramcontent.com/pod-product-compliance
Lightning Source LLC
Chambersburg PA
CBHW060508030426
42337CB00015B/1790